RESEARCH SUMMARY 1968-S1

Class Size

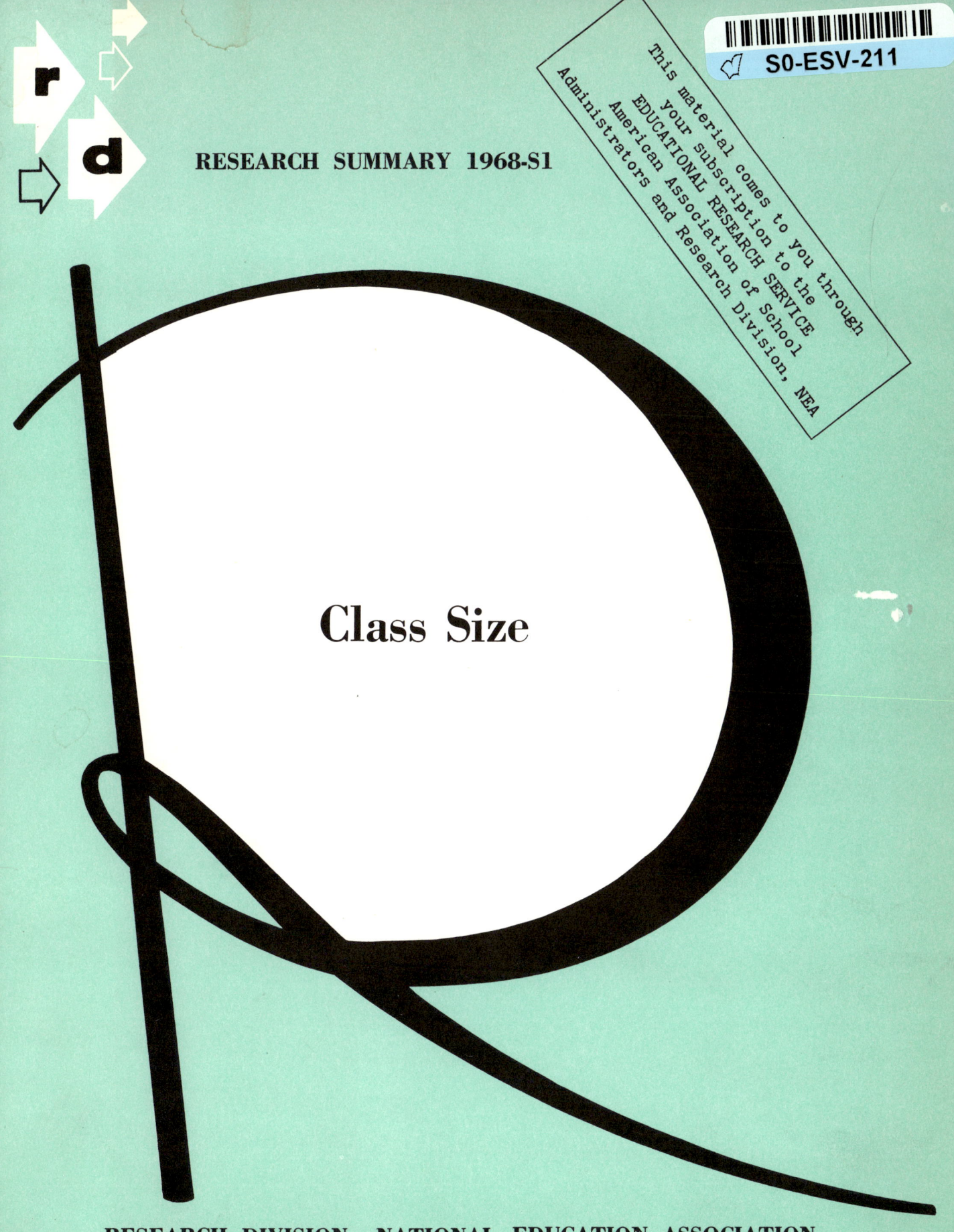

RESEARCH DIVISION – NATIONAL EDUCATION ASSOCIATION

RESEARCH SUMMARY 1968-S1

Class Size

RESEARCH DIVISION – NATIONAL EDUCATION ASSOCIATION

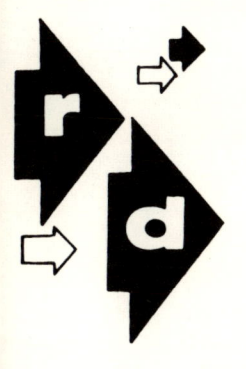

Copyright © 1968 by the
National Education Association
All Rights Reserved

NATIONAL EDUCATION ASSOCIATION

BRAULIO ALONSO, President
SAM M. LAMBERT, Executive Secretary
GLEN ROBINSON, Assistant Executive Secretary
    for Research

RESEARCH DIVISION

GLEN ROBINSON, Director

SIMEON P. TAYLOR III, Assistant Director and Chief of Statistics
WILLIAM S. GRAYBEAL, Assistant Director
ALTON B. SHERIDAN, Assistant Director
FRIEDA S. SHAPIRO, Assistant Director
ROBERT ASNARD, Assistant Director
EUGENE P. MC LOONE, Assistant Director

GERTRUDE N. STIEBER, Research Associate
NETTIE S. SHAPIRO, Research Associate

BEATRICE C. LEE, Publications Editor

VALDEANE RICE, Administrative Assistant

DONALD P. WALKER, Research Assistant
MARSHA A. REAM, Research Assistant
SHEILA MARTIN, Research Assistant
JOANNE H. BODLEY, Research Assistant
SHERRELL E. VARNER, Research Assistant
JEANETTE G. VAUGHAN, Research Assistant

GRACE BRUBAKER, Chief, Information
WALLY ANNE SLITER, Chief, Typing
FRANCES H. REYNOLDS, Chief, Library

RICHARD E. SCOTT, Associate Chief, Statistics
HELEN KOLODZIEY, Assistant Chief, Information
LILIAN YANG, Assistant Chief, Typing

Research Summary 1968-S1: CLASS SIZE
            Prepared by SHERRELL E. VARNER

Price of Summary: Single copy, $1.00. Stock #434-22810. Discounts on quantity orders: 2-9 copies, 10%; 10 or more copies, 20%. Orders may be billed but shipping charges will be added. Order from Publications Sales Section and make checks payable to the National Education Association, 1201 Sixteenth Street, N. W., Washington, D. C. 20036.

Reproduction: No part of this Summary may be reproduced in any form without written permission from the NEA Research Division, except by NEA Departments and affiliated associations. In all cases, reproduction of the Research Summary materials must include the usual credit line and the copyright notice.

Address communications to the Publications Editor, Research Division, National Education Association, 1201 Sixteenth Street, N. W., Washington, D. C. 20036.

Contents

Foreword 4

Overview 5

Introduction 5

Status and Trends 7

    Pupils per Classroom Teacher, by State 7
    Kindergarten and Elementary-School Class Size 7
    High-School Class Size 12
    Ethnic Origin and Class Size 12
    Size of School and Class Size 12

Research and Opinions 14

    The Teacher and Class Size 15
    Research on Class Size 18
    Previous Summaries of Research 19
    What Goes On in the Classroom? 20
    Kindergarten Classes 24
    Elementary-School Classes 24
    Junior High-School Classes 29
    High-School Classes 30
    Studies of Class Size in Other Countries 30
    Junior College and College Classes 31
    Future Class Size Research 33

Recommendations and Standards 34

    National Education Association 34
    Educational Policies Commission, NEA-AASA 34
    NEA Office of Professional Development and Welfare 35
    Association of Classroom Teachers, NEA 35
    Department of Elementary School Principals, NEA 36
    National Association of Secondary-School Principals, NEA 36
    American Association of School Administrators, NEA 37
    Association for Supervision and Curriculum Development, NEA 37
    NEA Project on the Instructional Program of the Public Schools 37
    Department of Elementary-Kindergarten-Nursery Education, NEA 37
    National Commission on Teacher Education and
        Professional Standards, NEA 38
    Association for Childhood Education International 38
    Standards Set by Regional Accrediting Agencies 38

School Board and Administrative Policy on Class Size and
    Teacher-Pupil Ratio 39

    Written Policies on Class Size 39
    Arriving at Class Size Policy 40

Teacher/School Board Negotiations on Class Size 41

References 45

Foreword

The proper sizes for classes have long concerned teachers, administrators, and laymen. The financial consequences of class size are obvious; the educational implications are less well defined.

Through the years since 1893, when the first research study of class size was published, many questions have been asked. How does the size of class affect the pupil, his achievement, his classroom behavior? How does size of class affect the teacher's morale, his teaching techniques, and his ability to individualize instruction? What should be given priority in establishing a school budget? Should funds be spent to employ more teachers in order to reduce sizes of classes? Or should teacher salaries be raised in order to attract and retain superior teachers? Or should funds be spent to employ such auxiliary professional personnel as counselors and reading consultants, or to employ nonprofessional teacher aides to assist teachers with nonteaching duties?

The continued relevance of an assessment of research on the topic can be seen in the growing number of negotiated agreements between teacher organizations and school boards containing provisions for class size. Its relevance is also evident in growing school enrollments, rising school construction costs, and the continued teacher shortage.

For these reasons this NEA Research Division has attempted in this Research Summary to survey and summarize research on class size in elementary and secondary schools. It has also attempted to identify the important issues and questions related to class size.

Readers should use caution in drawing final conclusions from the studies reported in this Research Summary. Many variables are present in the classroom learning environment, and most studies have attempted to control only a few of these variables. This survey of literature. demonstrates the need for further, carefully designed research on the many questions related to class size.

The summary has been prepared by Sherrell E. Varner, Research Assistant.

GLEN ROBINSON
Director, Research Division

CLASS SIZE

Overview

Is class size a significant factor in the learning environment of the one-teacher, self-contained classroom? Research has suggested that the adequacy of over-all staffing ratios (e.g., number of professional staff members per 1,000 pupils) and adequacy of teacher salaries are at least as important contributors to the learning environment and school quality as class size per se. Studies have shown that class size tends to affect teachers' feelings of effectiveness and their morale.

Can conclusions be drawn from existing class size research? Opinions have differed on this important question. The present survey suggests that it may not be so much that research is not conclusive, as many have thought, as it is that research has not been comprehensive. Many variables are present in the classroom environment--the pupils, the teacher, the subject matter, and the teaching methods, to name a few. Although the study of classroom environment is a multivariate problem, most class size research conducted to date has tended to use a single variable approach.

Research findings do not indicate that there is a one best class size, nor one best teacher-pupil ratio. However, it seems clear that in a small class a good teacher can devote more attention to individual pupils and their particular educational and emotional needs than the same teacher can devote in a substantially larger class. It appears that the teacher, his instructional methods, and his personal outlook are important factors that make a difference as class size varies. If the teacher approaches a small class just as he does a large class, the measurable differences between the two groups may be negligible. On the other hand, a teacher who is a master of effective techniques in instructing pupils in small classes can be completely frustrated and ineffective when faced with a large class.

In general, both opinion and research tend to agree that in order to produce optimal results--for both pupils and teachers--the size of class must be appropriate to the intellectual-emotional needs of the pupils, the skills of the teacher, the type of learning desired, and the nature of the subject matter.

The systems approach combined with multivariate analysis appears to hold promise in further study of the many unanswered questions pertaining to class size.

Introduction

The question of optimum class size, to paraphrase Keliher (31:3),[1]/ is a hardy perennial. Herodotus reportedly made reference to "classes of thirty." Many centuries later Comenius stated that "it is not only possible for one teacher to teach several hundred scholars at once, but it is also essential, since for both the teacher and students it is by far the most advantageous system." In contrast, John Locke, who was about 39 years old when Comenius died, thought that "it is impossible that the master shall have fifty or an hundred scholars--nor can it be expected that he instruct them properly in other than their books." (14:1-2)

Such divergent opinions came from educational philosophers and practitioners prior to 1893--when J. M. Rice reported the first "modern" research study on class size--just as the discussion continues today.

Class size is of perennial concern for at least two reasons. First, educators and laymen desire, and continue to seek, optimum learning conditions. Second, class size has tremendous impact on school finances.

The financial consequences of class size can be strikingly illustrated. Let us assume that in a medium-sized school system enrolling 15,000 pupils, the average class size is 30 pupils and the average teacher's salary is $7,000. A reduction in average class size from 30 to 29 pupils would require 17 additional teachers and a budget increase of $119,000 per year. If classes were reduced from 30 to 25 pupils per class, 100 additional teachers would be required. Teachers' salaries alone would add $700,000 to the annual budget requirements of this system.

The relationship between class size and optimal learning conditions is less well defined. Increased knowledge of individual differences and more sophisticated understanding of the learning process have negated the previous assumption that there is one "best" size for a class. The question now being asked is "Best class size for what ends and under what circumstances?" Included in this broad question are such considerations as the stated goals of education, the subject and type(s) of pupils

---

[1]/ Numbers in parentheses refer to items in the references at the end of this summary.

being taught, and the particular skills and interests of the individual teacher.

Some observers predict that because of the innumerable and unmeasurable variables present in the learning process and the learning environment, we probably shall never be able to determine even a desirable maximum class size. Others seem to imply that because of "newer" patterns of classroom organization, "newer" approaches to staff utilization and deployment, and the utilization of electronic teaching devices, the question of class size is becoming somewhat irrelevant.

However, class size continues to be of concern (beyond financial implications) to several interested groups--to citizens, who expect and demand the best possible returns on their tax dollars used for education; to parents, who want the best education for their children; to school administrators, who must administer policy decisions and allocate funds; and, most of all, to teachers, who are directly affected by class size.

Assuming for the moment the desirability of small classes, the decision to concentrate funds on salaries for additional teachers must be measured against several alternatives. Could funds be used better for one of the following:

1. To raise salaries in order to attract superior teachers

2. To hire extra-class professionals, such as subject-matter specialists, supervisors, and counselors

3. To hire nonprofessional personnel to relieve teachers from such nonteaching duties as supervising lunchrooms and playgrounds, and to perform such routine clerical tasks as scoring objective tests and recording grades

4. To purchase equipment and materials to change the present instructional procedures.

If the decision to hire more teachers in order to reduce class size stands, these teachers, who remain in short supply as school enrollment continues to increase, must be found. As part of a continuing series of studies of Teacher Supply and Demand in Public Schools, the NEA Research Division estimated that for the 1967-68 school year, 18,548 additional elementary-school teachers would be needed to reduce the maximum class size in all of our nation's elementary schools to no more than 34 pupils each. An estimated 7,915 additional secondary-school teachers would be required to reduce the maximum average daily teacher load to no more than 199 pupils.[2] In their publication, Class Size: The Multi-Million Dollar Question (70), Ross and McKenna asked these critical questions concerning the teacher shortage as it relates to class size: "How much should the certification rules be bent [in order to hire enough teachers to reduce class size]? How much of a chance should a school system take on an educational retread? Will the good that [smaller] classes [presumably] do be overbalanced by the damage done by a poor teacher?"

The class size question is of especial interest today for several reasons. First, increased responsibility has been given to education as a partial solution to many of our nation's social ills, particularly those of our urban areas. Reduced class size has been especially emphasized as a factor in the education of culturally disadvantaged children. The Head Start program, with its classes of 15 children to three adults, including one teacher, reportedly has been successful.

The importance of small classes and individual attention has also been emphasized in attempting to improve the education (and hopefully the lives) of residents of our central cities. Following an extensive investigation into the schools of a major Michigan city, an NEA special committee recommended to the Michigan legislature that the state program of school support provide for at least six specific educational improvements in depressed urban areas. One of the six recommendations was "reduce class size to approximately 15-20." (Others were provisions for master teachers, more specialists, and better health services, extension of the school day and year, and extension of the school program down to age three.)[3]

Another reason for current interest in class size is the experimentation with "new" methods of classroom organization and of staff utilization and deployment. Among these newer approaches which have implications for class size are cooperative or team teaching; nongrading; flexible scheduling, with large-group instruction, small-group activity, and independent study; use of sub- or para-professional personnel; and other arrangements for vertical and

---

[2] National Education Association, Research Division. Teacher Supply and Demand in Public Schools, 1967. Research Report 1967-R18. Washington, D. C.: the Association, 1967. 88 p. Estimates were based on data from a national survey of class size and teacher load in 1965-66.

[3] National Education Association, National Commission on Professional Rights and Responsibilities. Detroit, Michigan: A Study of Barriers to Equal Opportunity in a Large City. Washington, D. C.: the Commission, March 1967. p. 86-87.

horizontal grouping. Other recent trends which may affect the size of class are the use of educational television and experimentation with computer-assisted instruction.

A third reason for the current interest in class size is the rapid growth of professional negotiations. Class size is among the many elements of the instructional program now being negotiated between teacher organizations and school boards.

The importance of experimentation with, and the possible value of, new forms of classroom organization and staff utilization is recognized, but because the one-teacher, self-contained classroom still predominates, because written negotiations are including class size provisions, and because size of class in the larger consideration of optimum learning conditions is important, this summary has been prepared. The intent is not merely to summarize recent research, but also to point to some of the many issues and considerations surrounding the class size question. For the most part, the research is limited to studies on the one-teacher, self-contained elementary classroom and the departmentalized, but period-scheduled, secondary-school classroom. Sections of this summary will focus upon status, research and opinions, recommendations from professional organizations and standards set by regional accrediting agencies, school system policies, and written staff/school board agreements.

Status and Trends

The type of summary measure used to report class size statistics is not well established; data are obtained in several ways, and often yield differing results. Accurate, but also most time-consuming and least-often used, is a class-by-class count. Class size is frequently reported in terms of some measure of central tendency. The arithmetic mean, obtained by dividing the total number of pupils by the total number of classes, can be distorted by unusually large and unusually small classes. The number of pupils in the median class often gives a more accurate picture, and is sometimes accompanied by the first- and third-quartile figures. Range from smallest to largest class is sometimes reported, but mode is rarely given.

Basic to any attempt to deal with class size by using one of these measures of central tendency is the need to define class. Ross and McKenna suggest that a class is "any group of students scheduled to meet regularly for all or a definite fraction of a school day with one particular teacher for the purpose of learning or being instructed in some specific part of the school's curriculum." (70:3) This definition would include those classes which are usually large by reason of tradition (e.g., physical education classes) or content of the subject (e.g., choir and band classes), as well as those which are usually small by reason of the pupils being taught (e.g., special education classes for exceptional children). Were these classes to be included in determining "average" class size, some distortion would result.

Instead of using a measure of class size per se, some researchers have chosen a measure of numerical staff adequacy, i.e., the total number of pupils is measured against the total number of professional staff members, rather than against the total number of classes taught. Numerical staff adequacy is commonly reported in terms of either pupil-teacher ratio or the number of staff members per 1,000 pupils. Either measure requires definition of staff member. Are principals, librarians, department heads, supervisors, special teachers of music and art, nurse-teachers, homebound teachers, counselors, and other professional staff members to be included? The Metropolitan School Study Council, from which much class-size research has originated, has chosen to include all professional, licensed personnel in their definition of staff member. (70:3)

When viewing data which have been reported in terms of pupil-teacher ratio, care should be taken to determine whether the number of pupils has been measured against the number of classroom teachers or against the total number of professional staff. In order to avoid misinterpretation, perhaps the term pupil-teacher ratio should be replaced with the more precise terms pupil-classroom teacher ratio and pupil-professional staff ratio.

Pupils per Classroom Teacher, by State

Table 1 gives the most recent U. S. Office of Education figures for the average number of pupils per classroom teacher in public elementary and secondary schools, for the 50 states and for 15 large cities. In the fall of 1966, the national average was approximately 24 pupils per classroom teacher. State averages ranged from fewer than 19 pupils per classroom teacher in South Dakota to slightly more than 28 pupils per classroom teacher in Alabama. The range among the 15 large cities was from approximately 20 in New York City to nearly 30 in St. Louis.

Kindergarten and Elementary-School Class Size

The NEA Research Division periodically conducts surveys of class size in elementary schools. Data from these surveys of the years 1952-53 through 1964-65 are shown in Table 2. The trend over the 12-year period covered by the surveys has been toward decreased average class size.

TABLE 1.--PUPILS PER CLASSROOM TEACHER IN FULL-TIME PUBLIC ELEMENTARY AND SECONDARY DAY SCHOOLS, FOR 50 STATES AND 19 LARGE CITIES, FALL 1966

State and large city	Pupils per teacher	State and large city	Pupils per teacher
1	2	1	2
UNITED STATES	24.1	Ohio	25.9
		Oklahoma	24.2
Alabama	28.1	Oregon	21.8
Alaska	21.8	Pennsylvania	23.6
Arizona	23.4	Rhode Island	23.1
Arkansas	23.3	South Carolina	26.4
California	26.4	South Dakota	18.6
Colorado	22.7	Tennessee	27.3
Connecticut	23.0	Texas	24.2
Delaware	22.7	Utah	26.4
Florida	24.9	Vermont	21.1
Georgia	26.2	Virginia	24.1
Hawaii	25.8	Washington	26.0
Idaho	23.3	West Virginia	25.8
Illinois	23.0	Wisconsin[a]/	22.3
Indiana	24.5	Wyoming	19.7
Iowa	20.8		
Kansas[a]/	20.4		
Kentucky	25.3		
Louisiana	24.9		
Maine	20.5		
Maryland	23.7	Baltimore, Md.	25.4
Massachusetts	23.4	Boston, Mass.	23.0
Michigan	26.4	Chicago, Ill.	26.5
Minnesota	22.7	Cleveland, Ohio	28.2
Mississippi	28.0	Dallas, Texas	28.3
Missouri	25.3	Detroit, Mich.	28.7
Montana	21.3	District of Columbia	24.1
Nebraska	20.1	Houston, Texas	27.1
Nevada	24.0	Los Angeles, Calif.	28.1
New Hampshire	22.8	Milwaukee, Wis.[a]/	26.5
New Jersey	22.9	New Orleans, La.	26.4
New Mexico	23.4	New York, N. Y.	20.2
New York	20.6	Philadelphia, Pa.	26.4
North Carolina	25.0	San Francisco, Calif.	25.5
North Dakota	20.0	St. Louis, Mo.	29.7

Source:
  Hobson, Carol Joy, and Schloss, Samuel. *Fall 1966 Statistics of Public Elementary and Secondary Day Schools: Pupils, Teachers, Instruction Rooms, and Expenditures.* Washington, D.C.: Government Printing Service, 1967. p. 19.

  [a]/ Excludes vocational high schools not operated as part of the regular public school system.

The most recent nationwide NEA survey of kindergarten and elementary-school class size was made in 1965, and included a stratified sample of school systems enrolling 3,000 or more pupils. Returns came from 922 systems, or 89.1 percent, of the systems sampled. The data, shown in Table 3, are approximate, but may be regarded as fully representative of class size in all of the elementary schools in all public school systems enrolling 3,000 or more pupils. Excluded from the survey were special education classes, and physical education and other traditionally large classes.

Kindergarten classes--Given below are the estimated cumulative percents of pupils in kindergarten classes of certain designated sizes, and the estimated cumulative percents of kindergarten classes with designated numbers of pupils, in all systems enrolling 3,000 or more pupils as of March 1965.

Number of pupils per kindergarten class	Cumulative percents of totals	
	Classes	Pupils
More than 45	0.2%	0.4%
More than 40	1.0	1.6
More than 35	5.2	7.4
More than 30	25.7	32.1
More than 25	61.1	68.5

The data show that nearly 69 percent of kindergarten pupils attended classes enrolling more than 25 pupils. About 61 percent of all kindergarten classes in March 1965 enrolled more than 25 pupils. The estimated number of pupils in the median kindergarten class was 27, and in the mean kindergarten class, 27.2. (50:10-11)

Elementary classes--In March 1965, nearly 84 percent of all elementary-school pupils attended classes enrolling more than 25 pupils. Nearly 79 percent of all elementary classes enrolled more than 25 pupils. (50:13-14)

Number of pupils per elementary class	Cumulative percents of totals	
	Classes	Pupils
More than 45	0.4%	0.7%
More than 40	1.7	2.5
More than 35	10.0	13.1
More than 30	41.5	48.3
More than 25	78.7	83.9

For school systems enrolling 3,000 or more pupils, generally the larger the school system, the larger the typical elementary (including kindergarten) class is likely to be. This tendency can be seen in the data given in Table 3, which shows that in Stratum 1 systems (enrollment of 100,000 or more) 90.4 percent of pupils are enrolled in elementary classes having more than 25 pupils, while 77.6 percent of elementary pupils in Stratum 6 systems (3,000-5,999 pupils) are enrolled in classes having more than 25 pupils. Mean class size ranged from 28.4 pupils per class in the smallest systems surveyed to 31.6 pupils per class in the largest systems.

A more recent NEA Research Division study, The American Public-School Teacher, 1965-66 (49), reported the size of nondepartmentalized elementary classes. The median class size reported by the 1,105 responding teachers was 29 pupils, a figure slightly smaller than the 30 pupils found in the 1965 study (data shown in Table 3). The mean class size taught by the reporting teachers was 28.2, compared with 29.3 found in the earlier study.

Elementary and kindergarten class size by geographic region--Table 4 presents data for kindergarten and elementary-school pupils by geographic region. Some differences can be noted. As measured in terms of estimated cumulative

TABLE 2.--AVERAGE CLASS SIZE IN PUBLIC ELEMENTARY SCHOOLS, 1952-53 TO 1964-65

Year	Groups by population of school districts						Total
	100,000 or more	50,000-99,999	30,000-49,999	10,000-29,999	5,000-9,999	2,500-4,999	
1	2	3	4	5	6	7	8
1952-53	33.8	32.2	29.3	29.1	29.8	29.7	31.9
1955-56	32.9	31.5	29.3	29.3	28.9	29.0	30.4
1957-58	33.2	31.3	29.1	29.0	28.5	28.4	30.1
1959-60	32.0	30.5	28.6	28.2	28.1	27.6	29.5
	Strata by enrollment of school systems						
	100,000 or more	50,000-99,999	25,000-49,999	12,000-24,999	6,000-11,999	3,000-5,999	
1961-62	32.3	30.9	30.2	29.2	28.9	28.3	29.6
1964-65	31.6	30.1	29.5	29.2	28.6	28.4	29.3

Source:
National Education Association, Research Division. Class Size in Kindergartens and Elementary Schools, March 1965. Research Report 1965-R11. Washington, D.C.: the Association, July 1965. p. 12.

TABLE 3.--ESTIMATED PERCENT OF ELEMENTARY-SCHOOL PUPILS IN CLASSES IN EXCESS OF
CERTAIN DESIGNATED SIZES, AND MEDIAN AND MEAN CLASS SIZE, SCHOOL SYSTEMS
ENROLLING 3,000 OR MORE PUPILS, BY STRATA, MARCH 1965a/

Enrollment stratumb/	Total number of school systems	Estimated percent of pupils in classes in excess of					Number of pupils in	
		25 pupils	30 pupils	35 pupils	40 pupils	45 pupils	Median class	Mean class
1	2	3	4	5	6	7	8	9
1--100,000 or more pupils	21	90.4%	65.5%	20.8%	2.5%	0.4%	32	31.6
2--50,000-99,999 pupils	48	88.3	50.9	12.3	1.5	0.2	30	30.1
3--25,000-49,999 pupils	72	85.5	46.7	9.4	0.5	0.1	30	29.5
4--12,000-24,999 pupils	294	82.5	43.7	11.3	3.0	1.2	29	29.2
5--6,000-11,999 pupils	749	78.2	40.9	10.7	2.6	0.8	29	28.6
6--3,000-5,999 pupils	1,547	77.6	40.0	10.8	3.1	0.8	28	28.4
Total--3,000 or more pupils	2,731	82.5%	46.7%	12.6%	2.5%	0.7%	30	29.3
Total number of pupils involved	18,024,163	14,874,698	8,430,392	2,262,755	441,751	123,217		

Source:
National Education Association, Research Division. Class Size in Kindergarten and Elementary Schools, March 1965. Research Report 1965-R11. Washington, D.C.: the Association, July 1965. p. 13, 15.
a/ Includes grades K-6, K-7, K-8, depending upon the organization of the school system reporting.
b/ School systems are grouped according to enrollments reported in October 1963.

TABLE 4.--ESTIMATED PERCENT OF KINDERGARTEN AND ELEMENTARY SCHOOL PUPILS IN CLASSES IN EXCESS OF CERTAIN DESIGNATED SIZES, BY GEOGRAPHIC REGION, MARCH 1965[a]

Geographic region	\multicolumn{5}{c}{Estimated percent of pupils in classes in excess of}
	25 pupils	30 pupils	35 pupils	40 pupils	45 pupils
1	2	3	4	5	6
Northeast	74.7%	36.2%	8.8%	1.4%	0.2%
Southeast	85.6	53.4	17.8	5.1	1.8
Middle	83.3	47.1	11.7	1.4	0.2
West	85.7	49.1	11.3	1.7	0.3
Total	82.5%	46.8%	12.6%	2.5%	0.7%

Source:
National Education Association, Research Division. Class Size in Kindergartens and Elementary Schools, March 1965. Research Report 1965-R11. Washington, D.C.: the Association, July 1965. p. 15.

[a]/ Includes grades K-6, K-7, or K-8, depending upon the organization of the school system reporting.

TABLE 5.--MEDIAN CLASS SIZE IN JUNIOR HIGH SCHOOLS, AND PERCENT OF CLASSES WITH ENROLLMENTS BELOW 21 AND ABOVE 35, BY SUBJECT, 1963-64, SCHOOL SYSTEMS ENROLLING 12,000 OR MORE PUPILS

Subject	100,000 or more	50,000-99,999	25,000-49,999	12,000-24,999	Total	Below 21	Above 35
1	2	3	4	5	6	7	8
Art	32.0	29.9	28.4	27.9	29.3	12.8%	11.1%
Business	35.6	33.1	31.2	30.1	32.8	6.1	31.4
English	33.0	31.4	30.1	29.9	31.0	6.9	15.4
Foreign languages	32.5	28.7	27.3	26.1	28.0	19.1	11.5
Health and safety education	33.3	32.7	29.4	30.5	31.3	9.8	22.3
Physical education	38.7	38.0	35.3	34.8	36.6	8.3	52.0
Home economics	26.4	23.0	23.0	19.6	22.4	42.8	2.2
Industrial arts	26.1	24.0	23.2	20.2	22.9	39.8	1.7
Mathematics	33.6	31.7	30.4	30.2	31.4	5.3	17.1
Music	32.5	32.3	31.3	30.7	31.6	17.1	32.3
Science	33.9	31.8	30.7	30.4	31.5	4.3	17.2
Social studies	34.1	32.2	30.8	30.6	31.9	3.8	18.9
United (core)	...	31.4	33.8	30.3	31.5	4.2	13.4
Handicapped	19.4	16.3	12.1	13.6	16.8	76.8	0.5
Other	31.2	27.2	22.1	27.3	28.6	26.0	11.5
Total	32.7	31.2	29.9	29.2	30.6	12.7%	19.9%
Number of school systems in strata	21	48	73	301	443		
Number of school systems reporting on junior high schools	10	35	40	155	240		
Number of classes reported	79,322	92,300	58,294	121,104	351,020		

Source:
National Education Association, Research Division. Class Size in Secondary Schools, January 1964. Research Report 1964-R16. Washington, D.C.: the Association, December 1964. p. 14-15.

percents of pupils attending classes in excess of certain designated sizes, classes in schools in the Northeast are consistently the smallest, and classes in the Southeast schools are consistently the largest.

High-School Class Size

The most recent NEA Research Division survey of class size in secondary schools was conducted in January 1964. Table 5 gives data from that study on median class size in junior high schools by subject. Table 6 gives similar data for high schools. At the time of this study, the junior high-school median class size was consistently larger than the high-school median in academic subjects, while the reverse was generally true for vocational subjects. There was a steady decline in median class size from Stratum 1 (largest) through Stratum 4 (smallest surveyed in this study). In general, the larger the school system, the larger the classes in both junior high schools and high schools.

Ethnic Origin and Class Size

The U. S. Office of Education study entitled Equality of Educational Opportunity (popularly known as the Coleman report) (17) collected data on the average number of pupils per room for pupils of certain ethnic origin, by geographic location of the school. Data from that study are shown in Table 7.

Size of School and Class Size

In his study, School Size and Program Quality in Southern High Schools, Jackson (29) investigated class size, pupil-teacher ratio, and number of pupils taught daily. Included for study were 4,773 public high schools in 11 Southern states. Data were based on official records for the 1962-63 school year.

Size of classes--Generally, class size in high schools of all grade patterns (i.e., schools enrolling grades 7-12, 8-12, 9-12, or 10-12) increased up to school enrollments of 1,000;

TABLE 6.--MEDIAN CLASS SIZE IN HIGH SCHOOLS, AND PERCENT OF CLASSES WITH ENROLLMENT BELOW 21 AND ABOVE 35, BY SUBJECT, 1963-64, SCHOOL SYSTEMS ENROLLING 12,000 OR MORE PUPILS

Subject	100,000- or more	50,000- 99,999	25,000- 49,999	12,000- 24,999	Total	Below 21	Above 35
1	2	3	4	5	6	7	8
Art	29.0	28.3	26.0	23.3	26.9	22.7%	6.5%
Business	30.5	30.7	29.3	28.4	29.8	13.0	16.5
English	29.4	29.7	29.2	28.1	29.0	10.2	8.7
Foreign languages	28.6	27.4	26.0	25.0	26.6	22.7	6.2
Health and safety education	34.1	33.1	31.7	31.3	32.1	8.5	28.2
Physical education	42.9	37.6	37.8	36.6	38.8	6.7	59.1
Home economics	26.3	24.3	23.3	22.2	23.9	32.0	1.8
Industrial arts	26.1	24.1	23.3	21.2	23.5	33.8	1.5
Mathematics	31.0	29.6	29.0	28.1	29.2	10.1	9.7
Music	36.3	33.1	34.7	31.8	34.1	24.1	45.7
Science	31.0	29.5	28.7	27.9	29.1	9.4	7.9
Social studies	32.2	31.5	31.0	29.8	31.0	5.3	14.8
Driver education	22.5	18.3	18.1	22.3	21.1	49.8	15.9
Federally supported vocations	24.2	20.4	22.0	19.1	20.1	52.1	1.6
Other vocations	27.1	22.5	18.6	18.8	21.2	49.0	3.6
Handicapped	14.7	15.6	12.4	14.0	14.2	93.3	0.4
Other	36.5	26.4	29.3	19.0	30.1	25.6	26.5
Total	30.8	29.6	28.7	27.7	29.0	15.2%	15.7%
Number of school districts reporting	14	40	54	197	305		
Number of classes reported	108,095	112,289	88,163	154,580	463,127		

Source:
National Education Association, Research Division. Class Size in Secondary Schools, January 1964. Research Report 1964-R16. Washington, D.C.: the Association, December 1964. p. 18-19.

TABLE 7.--AVERAGE NUMBER OF PUPILS PER CLASSROOM[a]/ IN ELEMENTARY[b]/ AND SECONDARY[c]/ SCHOOLS, BY ETHNIC CLASSIFICATION OF PUPILS AND LOCATION OF SCHOOL, FALL 1965

Grade level and region	Negro	Majority (white)	Mexican-American	Puerto Rican	Indian-American	Oriental American
1	2	3	4	5	6	7
ELEMENTARY						
Whole nation	32	29	33	31	30	33
Nonmetropolitan						
North and West	25	28	*	*	*	*
South	34	26	*	*	*	*
Southwest	21	31	*	*	*	*
Metropolitan						
Northwest	33	30	*	*	*	*
Midwest	34	30	*	*	*	*
South	30	31	*	*	*	*
Southwest	39	26	*	*	*	*
West	37	31	*	*	*	*
SECONDARY						
Whole nation	34	31	32	33	29	32
Nonmetropolitan						
North and West	27	30	*	*	*	*
South	35	28	*	*	*	*
Southwest	22	20	*	*	*	*
Metropolitan						
Northwest	35	28	*	*	*	*
Midwest	54	33	*	*	*	*
South	30	34	*	*	*	*
Southwest	28	42	*	*	*	*
West	31	30	*	*	*	*

Source:
 Coleman, James S., and others. *Equality of Educational Opportunity.* U.S. Department of Health, Education, and Welfare, Office of Education. Washington, D.C.: Government Printing Office, 1966. p. 10, 11.
 * Data not reported.
 a/ Includes regular classrooms designed or remodeled for class instruction, laboratories and shops; excludes improvised or makeshift classrooms and general use facilities.
 b/ Based on data for sixth-grade pupils.
 c/ Based on data for twelfth-grade pupils.

no appreciable increases occured beyond this point. Class size was most nearly uniform in three-year high schools. The most pronounced fluctuations in class size were found in schools enrolling fewer than 500 pupils, while variations were less marked in schools enrolling more than 1,000 pupils. For example, median class size in all schools enrolling more than 1,000 pupils was approximately 28, while the median varied from 13 in schools having fewer than 100 pupils to 25 in schools enrolling 250-499 pupils. Jackson suggested that this finding was not unexpected, in light of the low enrollments in certain elective courses in the small high schools.

Pupil-teacher ratio--Pupil-teacher ratio was defined as "the numerical ratio between total school enrollment and total number of professional staff members assigned to a school." The ratio of pupils to teachers increased with an increased school size, up to the 500-999 pupil category. Changes beyond that point were not appreciable. Pupil-teacher ratio was quite low in small schools, especially in those enrolling fewer than 250 pupils.

Daily pupil load--The teacher's daily pupil load was derived for each group of schools with comparable enrollment and organizational pattern by dividing the total enrollment in all classes by the total number of teachers. Compared with those of teachers in large schools, daily pupil loads of teachers in small schools were relatively light. Basing calculations on the assumption that five classes per day is a normal teaching assignment, Jackson found that the classes taught by teachers in the smallest schools averaged 12-15 pupils, compared with 24-27 pupils in classes taught by teachers in the largest schools.

Research and Opinions

Pupils, teachers, administrators--all are affected by size of classes; the question of optimum size becomes "Best class size for what end, under what circumstances, for whom?" For the emotional growth of the pupils? For their intellectual growth? Most people probably would respond to both questions affirmatively.

Cohen (16:16-19) discussed class size in terms of behavioral differences which require that size of class be suitable to a teaching-learning style appropriate at different age levels. The first of the three student needs she outlined is the <u>emotional-social dependency of the learner on the teacher</u>. This need of the growing child, Cohen said, "can be met only by a human adult, and successful fulfillment at different stages in a learner's life may call for one class size rather than another as a learner shares the significant adult with others as needful as himself." The second need of the student is <u>cognitive-intellectual dependency on the teacher</u>--the student's dependency is shifted from the person who conveys the material to the material itself. The teacher's effectiveness in freeing children from unnecessary dependency on him as a sole resource, Cohen contended, "is surely related to the number of children with whom he must so interrelate, as well as to the stage of dependency of the children." Furthermore, "at certain points in the life of a learner, incorrect class size may <u>increase</u> rather than decrease dependency if a teacher is unable to guide and supervise the efforts at independence of too many children at the same time."[4]/ The third need is for <u>dependency on concrete and sensory nonverbal experience</u>. It involves "the ability of the learner to assimilate verbal presentation of unfamiliar content, a concomitant of age, experience and maturity." Cohen suggested that in assigning numbers of children to teachers, we need to know (a) how much direct contact of an active, physical, concrete character is needed for clarification of meaning at different levels of learner growth, (b) how much interaction with a significant adult is needed for the fulfillment of emotional and broadly variegated cognitive needs, and (c) with how many children at any given state of learning a teacher can cope.

Perhaps research could determine the numbers of pupils per classroom--for each type of pupil (e.g., ability, cultural background) at each age-need level and/or for each subject--that would maximize emotional and intellectual growth. Would these numbers apply equally well to all classrooms? To one classroom taught by a teacher who has lunchroom supervision responsibilities and no free period during the day, and to another in which the teacher has a duty-free lunch period and a daily 50-minute planning period? To one teacher who is an interesting and informed lecturer, and to another who is especially skilled at eliciting and directing small-group discussions? Where do the teacher's subjective feelings enter into the setting of class size(s)?

How can the administrator determine whether the positive results of reducing class size will offset the problems created by doing so? Does the desire to reduce class size justify going on split sessions or disrupting neighborhood loyalties by changing attendance areas? How can the administrator be certain that employing more teachers to reduce size of classes would result in a better learning environment than would employing more counselors, specialists, or paraprofessional teacher aides?

These are some of the many aspects of the class size question. After referring to the lack of definitive studies which establish a "best" class size, Shane (72) wrote:

> One is led to infer that the many different kinds of elementary and secondary classes, the varied characteristics of local communities, intellectual and temperamental differences among teachers, and the diverse nature of the subject matter between grade levels as well as within a grade level have made research on class size a problem that could be attacked only in a limited, qualified, or piecemeal fashion.

Some research which might be helpful has been done, however. The staff of the Metropolitan School Study Council has been especially interested in the comparative effects of <u>class size and numerical staffing adequacy</u> on <u>school</u> quality. Basing their conclusions on studies by McKenna (35) and Binion (9), Ross and McKenna reported that "numbers of nonclassroom, professional personnel are at least as important in predicting what is going to happen in a classroom as the actual class size." (70:12)

McKenna (35) found the correlation between "Growing Edge" scores (an evaluation instrument noting desirable educational practices) and total number of professional staff members per 1,000 pupils (numerical staffing adequacy) to be somewhat higher than the correlation between "Growing Edge" scores and average class size. Among a combination of quality-controlling factors of school systems, the quantity measure of staff which assisted most in predicting

---

[4]/ "Dependency and Class Size," by Dorothy Cohen. From CHILDHOOD EDUCATION, September 1966, Vol. 43, No. 1. By permission of the author and the Association for Childhood Education International, 3615 Wisconsin Avenue, N.W., Washington, D.C. 20016.

school quality scores was the total number of professional staff members. "The numerical adequacy measure made its strongest contribution when combined with adequate salaries for all staff and a sufficient amount of money to provide teachers with tools and clerical help." (70:13) McKenna concluded that the wisest administrative course would be to seek continuously "the best internal balance in the school system's budget of time and money--neither neglecting nor emphasizing, to the exclusion of all other considerations, the matters of number of professional persons to be employed and how they are to be assigned." (70:13)

Ross and McKenna (70:13) also reported Binion's conclusion (9) that "class size that deviates too markedly from that which might be expected of a system, knowing its expenditure position and spending pattern, tends to have a negative result."

Vincent, McKenna, and Swanson (78) cited a study of "up-to-dateness" of the school programs in 132 school systems in 33 states, a group selected from the membership of the Associated Public School Systems. Although incidental to the objective of the study, the results did shed some light on the question of numerical staffing adequacy versus high salaries. The researchers concluded that:

Salaries high enough to be competitive for personnel of high caliber is the crucial consideration. If a choice must be made between salaries and numerical staffing adequacy, it appears that the nod should go to competitive salaries. Thus, the choice of larger classes should be made only, if at all, as a tactic for paying higher salaries to obtain better teachers. (78:4)

Contained in the remainder of this section are the findings from several teacher polls on the subject of class size, followed by results of recent research studies on the subject. Concluding the section is a very brief discussion of some recently developed programs which have implications for the question of class size.

The Teacher and Class Size

Administrators and school boards with financing problems excluded, the classroom teacher is perhaps most immediately and directly affected by class size. The ways in which the teacher is affected are numerous. Each additional pupil places in the teacher's care another individual, one with unique learning patterns and problems to be discovered and dealt with, unique proficiencies to be challenged, unique interests to be explored, and with all the other special characteristics which make each child an individual in the classroom group. Each additional pupil contributes another paper to be checked, another examination to be scored, and several more questions to be considered. Each additional pupil also means a geometric compounding of the teacher's discipline and guidance problems. In a class with 10 pupils, the number of possible pupil-to-pupil relationships is 45. This number increases to 190 when 10 more children are added to the classroom. The number of possible inter-pupil relationships increases from 300 to 435 when class membership increases from 25 to 30.

Not all of these contributing factors may be objectively measured, but an observation of some consequences may be fairly objective--the teacher has only so much time; if the required work time, both in and out of the classroom, exceeds the amount of time available, someone or something suffers.

Other considerations of class size and/or teacher load are highly subjective; the teacher himself is a variable in the learning process. How a teacher feels about his teaching load, whether or not he experiences tension and strain, will in part reflect his working conditions. But the teacher's feelings will also reflect his personality. For example, the teacher may be perceptive of the needs of pupils, expert at diagnosis and prescription for learning problems and efficient in completing the necessary paperwork, so that he might well be able to handle a large class, but he feels he can deal more effectively with small groups than with large. How he feels toward the size of his class, his over-all load, and his work in general will surely affect his teaching. Other factors, such as health, relationships with his family and friends, and all of his life outside the classroom, will also be reflected in his attitudes toward his work.

In 1960 and 1962, the NEA Research Division (53:124) asked representative samples of teachers what they thought the best size was for most elementary school classes for effective teaching. They answered as follows:

	All teachers	Elementary-school teachers	Secondary-school teachers	Men teachers	Women teachers
Fewer than 20	18.9%	12.5%	27.6%	28.5%	14.4%
20-24 pupils	53.0	53.7	52.0	51.1	53.8
25-29 pupils	26.1	31.2	19.2	17.7	30.1
30-34 pupils	1.9	2.5	1.2	2.5	...
35 or more	0.1	0.1	...	0.2	1.7

In a 1967 national survey of teacher opinion the Research Division asked teachers: "Under which of the following conditions do you believe you could do the most effective job with students in your class or classes? (a) Class or classes of 25 to 30 pupils with the usual clerical and nonteaching duties to do yourself, or (b) Class or classes with 40 to 50 pupils with a full-time nonprofessional person to assist you with clerical work and nonteaching duties." The results of this poll overwhelmingly favored small classes:

	All teachers	Elementary-school teachers	Secondary-school teachers	Men teachers	Women teachers
Better job in small classes without help	83.6%	88.1%	78.5%	77.6%	86.6%
Better job in large classes with help	16.4	11.9	21.5	22.4	13.4

Otte (63) reported a study of a sample of elementary-school teachers and principals in 18 Indiana school systems. The questionnaire defined "creativity in teaching" as "teaching imaginatively, in a way that stimulates imaginative interaction between student and teacher,"5/ and asked the participants to indicate which of 13 factors fostered, and which of nine factors hampered, creativity. Judging from the agreement expressed by the 364 respondents (95 percent of those sampled), small class enrollment is one of the 12 factors fostering creativity in teaching. Otte reported that class size was especially noted by teachers as important; a greater percentage of teachers than of principals indicated agreement that creativity in teaching was fostered by small classes. (63:41)

California classroom teachers, according to one survey (71), favor state action to reduce class size. The survey, reported in 1965, was conducted by a Senate Committee of the State of California. About 75 percent of 30,000 California classroom teachers sampled returned questionnaires, which included the question, "Do you think it appropriate for the state to take action to reduce class size?" Eighty percent of elementary-school teachers and 78 percent of secondary-school teachers answered this question affirmatively. When responses of teachers in junior colleges and unified districts were also
_____
5/ "Creativity in Teaching," by Roy W. Otte. From CHILDHOOD EDUCATION, September 1966, Vol. 43, No. 1. By permission of the author and the Association for Childhood Education International, 3615 Wisconsin Avenue, N.W., Washington, D.C. 20016.

included, affirmative responses came from 81 percent of all responding teachers. (71:20)

Comprising the final section of this questionnaire was the open-ended question, "Is there any specific thing which you think calls for state action to help teachers do a better job of teaching?" Some teachers commented on only one condition, while others noted several. But the most frequently listed item was "smaller classes." One-fourth of all teachers mentioned smaller classes. By school levels, 27 percent of the responding elementary-school teachers, 22 percent of junior high-school teachers, 25 percent of the high-school teachers, and 12 percent of junior-college teachers believed the need for smaller classes called for state action. The next highest item was listed by 11 percent of the total number responding. (71:21-22)

Typical comments from these teachers were:

Reduce class load, reduce class load, REDUCE CLASS LOAD.... More teachers leave the teaching profession for this one reason than any other--even skinflint salaries.

There are other problems that could be mentioned, but this problem is so preeminent that I won't even mention them for fear of detracting from American education's No. 1 problem.   --Junior high-school teacher

The class load is too large.... I feel my best teaching was done the year I had 23 students. There was time to answer everyone's questions and more individual help was given.

It is very disheartening to send the class home at the end of the day, knowing someone has a question unanswered, or someone doesn't quite understand the assignment. It is impossible to sit down with every child for more than a minute or two, because our time schedule is too full. --Elementary-school teacher

Class size and teacher load: appropriate class sizes should be determined for each subject area or grade level, and maximum teacher loads should likewise be determined for each area.   --High-school teacher

One of the most comprehensive, recent studies of the teacher and class size was included as a part of the NEA Research Division study of The American Public-School Teacher, 1965-66. (49:28-29) The results of this study were based on a 92.7 percent return from 2,528 classroom teachers identified in a two-stage sample. Of interest to this summary were responses to questions about size of class(es) taught, evaluation of present teaching load, and feelings of strain or tension in work.

To the question, "How would you describe your present teaching load?" the majority (62.3 percent) of teachers replied "reasonable," while 31.0 percent said "heavy," and 6.7 percent said "extremely heavy." Analysis of the differences among groups of teachers in the percents reporting heavy or extremely heavy teaching loads showed no statistically significant differences between (a) men and women, (b) single women and married women, (c) those with bachelor's degrees and those with master's degrees, and (d) elementary-school and secondary-school teachers. Nor were there differences on the basis of size of school system. There were differences on the basis of experience, however. The group of teachers with less than three years of experience included relatively fewer reporting heavy or extreme loads than was true of other experience groups.

There was also a strong relationship between number of pupils taught and the teacher's evaluation of his present teaching load, as the data in Table 8 show. Elementary-school teachers reporting heavy or extreme loads included 26.4 percent of those having classes of fewer than 25 pupils and 51.5 percent of those with classes of 30 or more pupils. Secondary-school teachers reporting heavy or extreme loads included 27.4 percent of those having fewer than 115 pupils per day and 49.8 percent of those teaching 150 or more pupils per day. (49:28)

To the question, "How would you describe your feelings of strain or tension in your work?" about 84 percent of the teachers reported they were experiencing little or moderate strain, and about 16 percent reported considerable strain or tension in their work. By whatever grouping, a majority of each group reported little or moderate strain. Significant variations did appear, however, in the size of minorities that reported considerable strain. The subgroups that were significantly below one or more of the other subgroups in the same category, in the percent reporting considerable strain, were:

Teachers in the Northeast, in contrast with those in the middle region

Teachers with bachelor's degrees, in contrast with those with master's degrees

Teachers under 30 years of age, in contrast with those in all other age groups

Teachers with less than three years of teaching experience, in contrast with those in all other experience groups

Teachers in middle-sized school systems (3,000-24,999 pupils), in contrast with those in all other size systems.

Other groupings of teachers in which differences appeared in the percent reporting considerable strain were: (a) number of teachers in elementary school, (b) number of teachers in secondary school, and (c) number of hours per week in all teaching duties.

Only three groupings showed a consistent relationship between the factor being measured and the percent of teachers reporting considerable strain:

TABLE 8.--EVALUATION OF PRESENT TEACHING LOAD, BY NUMBER OF PUPILS TAUGHT

Evaluation of teaching load	Elementary-school teachers, by size of class					Secondary-school teachers, by average number of pupils taught per day				
	All reporting	Fewer than 25	25-29	30-45	30 or more (includes column 5)	All reporting	Fewer than 115	115-149	150-184	150 or more (includes column 10)
1	2	3	4	5	6	7	8	9	10	11
Reasonable load	61.7%	73.6%	74.0%	55.5%	48.5%	62.9%	72.6%	65.1%	55.6%	50.2%
Heavy load	30.9	21.6	21.2	38.9	41.4	31.1	23.0	29.3	36.5	39.8
Extremely heavy load	7.3	4.8	4.7	5.6	10.1	6.0	4.4	5.6	7.9	10.0
	99.9%	100.0%	99.9%	100.0%	100.0%	100.0%	100.0%	100.0%	100.0%	100.0%
Number reporting .	1,202[a]	269	358	337	575	1,091[a]	365	341	266	410

Source:
National Education Association, Research Division. *The American Public-School Teacher, 1965-66.* Research Report 1967-R4. Washington, D. C.: the Association, 1967. p. 28.
[a] Includes those not reporting on number of pupils.

Group of teachers	Number reporting	Little strain	Considerable strain
All teachers reporting.	2,290	22.1%	16.2%
Number of pupils in elementary-school class			
Fewer than 25 pupils.	267	25.8	11.6
25-29 pupils	358	28.5	12.8
30-34 pupils	338	16.0	18.6
30 or more (includes preceding item)....	573	17.6	20.6
Teacher's estimate of teaching load			
Reasonable	1,425	30.2	7.6
Heavy	709	9.3	26.0
Heavy or extremely heavy (includes preceding item)....	861	8.6	30.6
Teaching time spent out of major field			
None; teaching in major field only ..	1,576	22.9	15.1
Some but less than 50 percent	300	23.0	17.7
50 percent or more ..	364	16.8	20.0

Data from this 1965 NEA Research Division study indicate a strong relationship between number of pupils taught and the teacher's evaluation of his teaching load, and a consistent, though less significant, relationship between numbers of pupils taught by the elementary-school teacher and the teacher's feelings of considerable tension and strain in his work.

Research on Class Size

Class size studies have lacked uniformity and, especially in the earlier studies, scientific controls. In viewing class size research, three problems must first be dealt with: definition of terms, criterion, and research situation.

1. *Definition of terms.* Mentioned in a previous section were the needs to define "a class" and to differentiate among mean and median class size, classroom teacher-pupil ratio, and numerical staff adequacy as measured either by professional staff-pupil ratio or by number of professional staff members per 1,000 pupils. Also to be dealt with is the need to define a "small class" and a "large class." The numbers of pupils which have been studied in "small" and "large" classes have varied considerably from study to study. For example, Stevenson (75) cited a 1909 study which differentiated between small classes enrolling fewer than 40 pupils and large classes enrolling 50 or more pupils. Another study divided classes into those enrolling 50 or fewer pupils and those enrolling more than 50. Still other research cited by Stevenson studied small classes of 30-34 pupils, of 20 or fewer pupils, and of 10 or fewer pupils. Such wide variations in numbers enrolled in "small" and "large" classes necessitates cautious study-to-study comparisons.

Another factor to consider is the spread between small and large classes. Would the conclusions drawn from comparing small classes of 30 or fewer with large classes of more than 30 be as valid as conclusions based on a study comparing small classes of 20 or fewer with large classes of 30 or more pupils? In the first case one additional pupil could possibly separate small classes from large, compared with nine pupils in the second case.

2. *Criterion.* This involves the question of what shall be measured in the study--the effects of class size on pupil retention? on pupil achievement? on teacher creativity? This recalls the old and basic question: "What are the goals for education?"

In their summary for the 1950 edition of the *Encyclopedia of Educational Research* (61), Otto and von Borgersrode outlined five stages through which the investigation of class size has passed. During the first stage, termed the "pioneer period" (approximately 1895-1915), the criteria used to measure the effects of class size were such administrative records as promotion rates, pupil withdrawals, pupil conduct, and classroom management; personal observations; and pupil achievement as measured by improvised subject-matter tests. No factor except class size was controlled in these studies. During the "early experimental period" (1916-1919), researchers attempted to hold constant some of the many variables in a given situation, and administered unstandardized objective tests to pupils in classes of various sizes. During the next, or "controlled-experimental," stage (1920-1924) intelligence and achievement were measured in controlled and semicontrolled experiments, by means of standardized instruments. Otto and von Borgersrode reported that none of the research completed during the first three stages provided any clear evidence of the superiority of small classes. During the very brief fourth stage (1925) researchers attempted to test the thesis that special techniques of instruction appropriate to classes of various sizes would make a difference in the results. More specific factors, such as pupil attitudes and teacher knowledge of individual pupils, were the criteria in studies during the years 1926-1937, characterized as a period of "refined experimentation."

Otto and von Borgersrode's summary illustrated the great variety of criteria that were used in early studies. Although refined research techniques, improved measurement instruments, and redefined goals of education have resulted in some changes, recent research studies have continued to measure the effects of class size against many criteria.

3. *Research situation*. The research situation abounds with such variables as type of pupil studied (e.g., academically talented or "slow learners"), type of teacher involved (e.g., superior or inferior), and subject being studied (e.g., algebra or American History). Because each classroom presents a unique set of variables, generalizations from research results and application of the results to a particular classroom must be done cautiously.

One relevant problem derives from an effort to control the quality, type, and method of teaching in the research situation. Some studies attempt to control these first two variables by comparing a small and a large class taught by the same teacher. This teacher, however, may be particularly skilled in working with large groups, or he may be biased against the effectiveness of large classes. Suppose the latter were the case, and the results of the study favored the small class. Might the results have been reversed if the teacher, as first described, had been better equipped to teach the large class than the small?

Other researchers attempt to control the third variable by instructing the teacher to use the same methods of teaching in the different-sized classes. Suppose that on the criterion of achievement, these large and small classes showed no significant differences. Might differences have appeared if the classes had been taught by methods appropriate to the class sizes? In the conclusion of his summary of four studies, which revealed few significant differences (statistical or otherwise) between large and small classes, Otto (65:155) wrote:

> The class-size problem has not been resolved. The present study, plus those previously completed, merely indicates that small classes <u>as now taught</u> do not harbor in significant proportion their purported advantages over large classes. If the physical environment of classrooms, curriculum, method, child study procedures, and home-school relations were tailored to be specifically suitable to small and large classes, it might be possible to demonstrate a geniune superiority for small classes.

Previous Summaries of Research

Blake (10) analyzed writings published prior to 1950. Of the 250-plus documents located, he eliminated (a) those which dealt with grade levels or institutions other than public elementary and secondary schools, and (b) those which were status reports, exhortations, testimonials, philosophical discussions, etc., rather than original research. The conclusions of the 85 studies which met this definition were as follows: the smaller the better, 35; the larger the better, 18; author would not claim he had made a case either way, 32. When the inconclusive studies were eliminated, the studies favored small classes over large in a ratio of two to one.

Blake further analyzed the studies for acceptability by setting six criteria: scientific control, adequacy of sample, adequacy of measurement of variable, adequacy of measurement of criterion, rigorousness of examination of data, and appropriateness of the conclusions. Only 22 of the 85 studies met these "minimum standards" and could be considered "scientific" research. Sixteen favored small classes, three favored large classes, and three were inconclusive. Eliminating the inconclusives, the ratio of studies favoring small over large classes strengthened to five to one.

Holland and Galfo (27) reported in 1964 an investigation "to determine what conclusions and implications might be drawn from an analysis of research concerning class size." The analysis was limited to that literature in which (a) the author had identified an area to be investigated, (b) data were collected and analyzed in a systematic manner, and (c) conclusions were drawn in terms of the data collected.

It was concluded that

1. There is no optimum class size, nor is there a perfect teacher-pupil ratio.

   a. Regardless of how the research is divided for analytical purposes--by grade level, subject, experimental design, or historically--the results are inconsistent. Either the research designs were uniformly invalid or else variables other than size of class were operating to produce learning results.

   b. Even in cases limited to achievement alone, standardized testing showed inconsistent results.

   c. There seems ample evidence . . . that when the learning objectives include the development of desirable attitudes and behavior patterns as well as subject matter content the classes should be small. Here, too, there is no perfect class size nor teacher-pupil ratio. But the smaller classes proved more effective when the learning outcomes were measured by a variety of techniques supplementing standardized subject matter tests.

   > In connection with the generalization, it should be pointed out that "small class size" is a vague concept. Research indicates that "small" has reference to the number of pupils that can make up a group in which each

member can react to other group members and to the teacher.... The evidence indicated that no group size is so small that it causes a perceptible decline in learning. (27:19)

2. The proper class size is a function of many factors, including course objectives, nature of the subject matter, nature of the teaching process used, and teacher understanding and morale, among others.

3. More important to learning than any fixed teacher-pupil ratio are the "ability of the teacher as a classroom practitioner and his willingness to be flexible in his approach to teaching."

   a. It is impossible to control "the contribution of a talented and devoted teacher to large or small class learning."

   b. Generally, teachers prefer small classes.

   c. "In instances where large class ratios proved to be superior to, or as effective as, small class ratios, the teachers had been given special training, special motivation or recognition for handling a large class. [Often] superior teachers were selected for both the experimental and control classes."

4. Over-all staff-pupil ratio is more important than teacher-pupil ratio.

   a. When numbers of pupils per teacher are increased, learning is increased only when the teacher is assisted by nonteaching personnel.

   b. Studies of the use of teacher aides, lay readers, self-instructional devices, team teachers, released time for teachers of large classes, and use of teacher assistants show improved learning outcomes with large numbers of learners to one master teacher.

   c. When a teacher has little or no help in handling large classes, discipline problems become more numerous and teacher morale suffers.

   d. Learning in large groups can be effective provided (a) the teacher is trained and motivated, (b) there is an opportunity for small group work to meet objectives not fulfilled in large classes, and (c) school facilities and schedules are kept flexible.

Holland and Galfo noted that class size research may be divided in several ways: historically, by grade level, subject, or criterion. In this summary, recent research has been organized first by criterion--studies that deal generally with what goes on in the classroom--and later by grade level.

What Goes On in the Classroom?

Adoption of inventions and newer practices--Clarence Newell (59) first used the ability of a school to adopt "newer practices" (e.g., field trips, school gardens, informal seating, individualized instruction) as a criterion in assessing the effects of class size. The basic premise of this study, which was reported in 1943, was that children get better educational experiences when teachers use new and promising practices. Newell's question was, "Do large or small classes provide a better setting for invention and early diffusion of newer educational practices?" Ross and McKenna, in their study, Class Size: The Multi-Million Dollar Question, (70:7-8) reported Newell's findings:

1. Teachers of small classes invent more new practices.

2. New practices invented by others tend to be taken on more readily in small classes.

3. Small classes are no guarantee of adaptability. Many other conditions exert an influence, and not the least among these is the quality of the personnel employed.

4. There is no evidence that money for small classes is better than money for better teachers.

5. Therefore, only when a capable teaching staff has been secured will small classes produce the kinds of results that are expected of small classes.

Ross and McKenna concluded their summary of this study by stating that "given [a] generally competent staff, the smaller the classes the greater the chances for inventions and early adoptions of newer and better practices". (70:8)

Use of desirable techniques--Harold Richman (68) used a checklist of selected classroom practices to investigate the effects of larger and smaller classes on the frequency of use of 62 desirable techniques. Included for study were middle elementary grades in school systems which had, by administrative decision and policy, deliberately decreased or increased class size. Ross and McKenna (70:8-9) reported that Richman

found consistent evidence that in the school systems where class size had been deliberately reduced, practices designed to produce greater teacher understanding of individuals, their aptitudes, and needs were increasingly used. The same was found in regard to practices designed to increase tailor-made instruction for all children, including atypical children, to discover and foster individual talents, and to encourage intellectual exploration through books, science experiments, and other sources of insight.

Conversely, Richman found that "where class size had been increased, these same kinds of practices were used with less frequency and consistency." He also discovered that

> where the teachers were aware of the reduced class-size policy and had been asked to give definite attention to taking advantage of the better situation, results came more quickly and were more pronounced than in those situations where the teachers were not let in on the policy decision. Where class size had been increased and the teachers had been informed of the inevitability and imminence of this change, had been asked to give some thought to reducing the negative effects expected, and had offered help by supervisory and administrative personnel to find ways of easing the methodological adjustment, the loss in good practice was not as great as where nothing had been done except to assign more pupils to each teacher. Richman also found that there is probably as much as a three-year lag in teachers' adjusting to the advantages of small classes. (70:9)

The over-all conclusion of Richman's study was that when class size is increased, desirable classroom practices tend to be dropped, while the reverse occurs when class size is reduced.

Variety of instructional methods--Whitsitt (80) observed the instructional methods used by teachers in over 60 large (more than 33 pupils) and small (fewer than 24 pupils) high school social studies and English classes. The classes were taught by equated teachers in 35 comparable school systems. Ross and McKenna reported that

> Whitsitt found that on every criterion of his observation schedule, the small classes had the advantage over the large classes. In all small classes there was more group work, more informality, and more opportunity for interaction of all kinds. Most small classes used some enrichment materials beyond the textbook, while three-fourths of the large classes were totally textbook classes. He found that the typical small class utilized dramatizations, special publications, and similar devices to make subject matter concrete more often than did large classes, although there was no real, insurmountable obstacle to using these practices in the larger class situations. Similarly, the subject matter covered was more detailed and current in small classes than large--study of such things as corporation stocks, fair employment practices, and public education as an aspect of governmental services--even though size of class should not, in itself, set greater or lesser limitations on what the textbook or established syllabi covered. (70:9-10)

The conclusion drawn from this study was that high-school classes that are small by design, rather than by accident, tend to have more variety in instructional methods than do large classes.

Individualization of attention--Ross and McKenna (70:10) suggested that "the strongest argument for small classes is that they prevent 'educational accidents.'" They base their generalization that more attention to individuals is likely to be found in small classes on studies by Richman, Whitsitt, Pertsch, and McKenna.

Richman (68) found that teachers of small classes not only knew the pupils in their classes as individuals, but also used the knowledge as a basis for action. Whitsitt's (80) study revealed that teachers in half of the small high-school classes, but only 6 percent of teachers of large high-school classes, provided for simultaneous, different assignments based on the particular needs of individual pupils.

Pertsch (66) studied 100 New York City elementary schools. Results of a 15-item test of teacher knowledge of their pupils' mentality, school history, health history, and family background revealed that teachers of small classes knew more about the individual pupils in their classes than did teachers of large classes. Pertsch also found that individualized instruction in reading and arithmetic was used more frequently in small than in large classes.

McKenna (35) compared class size data of school systems which had been evaluated by the "Growing Edge," an instrument published and used by the Metropolitan School Study Council and basically a checklist of desirable educational practices. Ross and McKenna reported the results:

> Teachers in small-class elementary schools were more often found observing children at work and making a record of their individual interests. In these systems, cumulative records more often contained statements of outstanding accomplishments and successes of each pupil, and more teachers discussed special interests and aptitudes of children during home conferences. Children who had shown exceptional talents had been given opportunities to develop these talents with extensive personal supervision by a teacher. Where study under private instruction could be helpful in the development of these special talents (e.g., private music lessons), adjustments in the curriculum were more often made to allow such study.

The advantages of small classes on the high school level were found to be much less pronounced than in the elementary schools. However, similar trends were noticeable and, in particular, greater home-school-community interaction occurred to provide the best help, guidance, and service for individual children. (70:11)

Pugh (67) reported a study made in the spring of 1963 by the Commission on the 1980 School, of the Metropolitan School Study Council. The specific concern of the study was to compare the kinds of teaching and learning procedures that occur in small and large classes. Ten experienced educators, who had been specially instructed in classroom observation techniques for this study, used a common guide to make half-hour observations in classrooms in nine school districts. Each observer limited his observations to two in the same class. Providing that the present class size was the result of a gradual increase or decrease rather than a sudden change, classes were selected at random. Observers were instructed to match subject areas wherever possible (e.g., to observe one large and one small class in reading).

Large classes were those having 30 or more pupils; small classes were those enrolling 20 or fewer pupils. Large classes ranged in size from 30 to 43 pupils, with a median of 31. Small classes ranged in size from 10 to 20 pupils, with a median of 18.

A total of 180 observations was made--90 in large classes and 90 in small. For both large and small classes, 30 observations were made in the primary grades (K-3), 30 in the intermediate grades (4-6), and 30 in the secondary grades (7-12).

The observation guide focused on "the degree of individualization in the teaching function." Individualization of instruction was described as a situation in which "the teacher has a knowledge of the needs, interests, and abilities of individual pupils and designs the instruction so as to meet these differences through the use of diagnostic tests, guidance records, et cetera." A list of 16 learning activities was compiled, and it was assumed by observers that whenever the pupils were engaged in one or more of the learning activities, they were learning. As each incident of learning was observed, it was noted by the numbers of pupils involved. The size of groups were as follows: individual (1-4 pupils involved), small group (5-9 pupils), or mass (10 or more pupils).

Comparisons were made between small and large classes on the basis of (a) frequency of learning activities taking place on an individual basis, (b) arrangements for individualized instruction versus mass instruction, (c) variety of learning activities and (d) frequency of the practices employed by teachers for the purpose of individualizing instruction.

The results of this study are given below:

1. <u>Frequency of learning activities taking place on an individual basis</u>--A far greater percentage of individual (1-4 pupils) and small group (5-9 pupils) activities were found in small classes than in large classes. Conversely, a far greater percentage of mass instruction (involving 10 or more pupils) activities were found in large classes than in small. Although there was a high degree of concern for

TABLE 9.--DISTRIBUTION OF LEARNING ACTIVITIES BY SIZE OF PUPIL-GROUP IN LARGE AND SMALL CLASSES

Size of group	Classes of 20 or fewer pupils				Classes of 30 or more pupils			
	Primary, K-3	Intermediate, 4-6	Secondary, 7-12	Total, K-12	Primary, K-3	Intermediate, 4-6	Secondary, 7-12	Total, K-12
1	2	3	4	5	6	7	8	9
1-4 pupils	52%	45%	27%	41%	24%	26%	20%	23%
5-9 pupils	13	10	23	16	14	4	7	9
10 or more pupils	35	45	50	43	62	70	72	68
Total number of activities observed	265	278	272	815	280	156	243	679

Source:
Pugh, James B. <u>The Performance of Teachers and Pupils in Small Classes</u>. Metropolitan School Study Council, Commission on the School of 1980, Commission Study No. 1. New York: Institute of Administrative Research, Teachers College, Columbia University, 1965. p. 29-36.

the individual pupil in small classes, a considerable amount of instruction in these classes was mass-oriented. For both large- and small-class groups, the greatest concern for the individual pupil occurred at the primary level.

Table 9 provides some of the data on which these conclusions were based. It shows that the percentage of observed learning activities occurring in groups of 1-4 pupils in the 90 small classes was 41 percent, compared with 23 percent in the 90 large classes. Small-group instruction was also more prevalent in small classes than in large, but the situation was reversed for mass instruction. While summary comparisons favored small classes for individual and small group activities, changes in the pattern appeared as differences were viewed by school level.

In comparing the number of learning activities occurring in small and large classes, the median fell into the 5-9 pupil grouping in small intermediate and secondary classes, while in small primary classes, the median fell in the 1-4 pupil grouping. The median for large classes at all three grade levels fell in the 10-or-more-pupils category.

Pugh noted, however, that even in small classes much instruction involved 10 or more pupils. Forty-three percent of the learning activities in the 90 small classes occurred in these "mass" groups, with 50 percent of the instruction in small secondary classes occurring in these large groups. As data in Table 9 show, the comparable percentages for large classes were much higher.

2. <u>Arrangements for individualized versus mass instruction</u>--Given below is the number of classes in which arrangements for individualized instruction were made. These figures also show that such arrangements were found in more small classes than large, and were found in more primary classes, both large and small, than in intermediate and secondary classes of comparable size. (67:37)

	Arrangements for individualized instruction	No arrangements for individualized instruction
Classes of 20 or fewer pupils		
Primary	20	10
Intermediate	15	15
Secondary	13	17
Total	48	42
Classes of 30 or more pupils		
Primary	10	20
Intermediate	9	21
Secondary	7	23
Total	26	64

In small classes there were 249 incidents of instruction involving only one pupil and in large classes, only 86. Further analysis revealed that 30 percent of all learning activities in small classes involved only one pupil, compared with 13 percent in large classes.

3. <u>Variety of learning activities</u>--In this study teachers of both large and small classes relied heavily on four of the 16 learning activities--listening, reading, recalling, and observing. These four activities represented 51 percent of all learning activities taking place in the 90 small classes, and 64 percent of all learning activities observed in the 90 large classes. Analysis found statistically significant differences, all favoring small classes, in seven of the 16 learning activities--listening, executing manipulative or motor skills, developing or practicing reading skills, outlining, generalizing, analyzing, and creating.

It was also found that within a given period of time a greater variety of activities takes place in small classes than in large.

4. <u>Frequency of the practices employed by the teacher for the purpose of individualizing instruction</u>--A total of 164 teaching practices used to individualize instruction were observed. Of these, 110 were observed in small classes, and 54 in large. When the 180 classes were analyzed together, 69 of the 164 practices were reported at the primary level, 55 at the intermediate level, and 40 at the secondary level.

Pugh concluded that "greater attention to individual differences occurs where the class size is small enough to enable the teacher to assume the responsibility for the learning of all pupils to their greatest potential."

<u>Teacher morale</u>--Harap (25) summarized results of a 10-year study to discover what factors affect teacher morale. Teachers in 20 school systems were interviewed during the years 1947-1957. Although many factors affected the morale of these teachers, their responses indicated that a good salary scale and reasonably small classes were the most important factors fostering job satisfaction and high morale. Discontent was focused chiefly on large classes, poor buildings, and the lack of a rest period, especially among elementary-school teachers. Harap concluded that class size was one of the most important factors that shape the teacher's attitude toward his work, and that a large class does more to destroy the teacher's confidence than any other single factor.

<u>Group dynamics</u>--Some research in the area of group dynamics seems relevant to the question of class size.

Bovard (11) in 1951 reported the results of an experiment contrasting classroom interaction in a group-centered class and in a leader-centered class. In the group-centered class, student-to-student interaction was fostered by a number of specific techniques; in the leader-centered class, student-to-student interaction was firmly limited, and verbal interaction was channeled between teacher and individual pupil. At the end of the test period, the leader-centered class showed almost none of the spontaneity, initiative, or cohesion of the group-centered class. Bovard concluded that the amount of good fellowship and cohesion, as well as initiative, in small, face-to-face groups is related to the amount of social interaction among group members.

The relevance of his conclusion to the question of class size rests in the possibility that even when deliberate efforts are made in large classes to provide for student interaction, the class may still be leader-centered. Its very bigness makes such an organization easier, if not inevitable.

Also important to the consideration of class size are some findings which have come from work in group processes. Two requirements for maximum individual growth in the classroom have been formulated: (a) Children should possess sufficient academic skill so that they can perform increasingly difficult and diversified tasks. (b) A group should possess sufficient social skill so that its efforts can be coordinated toward group goals. What size of group is necessary to meet these requirements?

Leton (33) stated that a class should be composed of the smallest number with which it is possible to obtain all the social and academic skills necessary for solving a problem. A class larger than necessary results in "frustration in the child's academic and social development." In classes larger than the necessary minimum, there is less need for pupils to assume responsibility because of an overlapping of skills, and individual contributions are less significant. There is, consequently, less drive to participate, and the "opportunities for the experimental acts from which behavior codes and moral standards are built" are decreased.

Kindergarten Classes

Cannon (13) studied the effects of class size on kindergarten groups. Included for study were one large class (enrollment ranged from 34 to 39 pupils) and one small class (enrollment ranged from 23 to 28 pupils) taught by one teacher who used the same program, procedures, room, and equipment for both classes. Observations were made in five areas:

1. <u>Aggressive acts</u>, such as pushing, bumping, crowding, and striking, were observed more often in large than in small groups.

2. <u>Peer relationships</u> were more favorable in small groups. Cannon reported that small-group children made friends more easily, had a sense of belonging, felt more secure, adjusted to group living more readily, and helped one another. More small-group than large-group children were able to make several friends and depend less upon one friend.

3. The quality of classroom living, as indicated by the <u>number and quality of child-teacher contacts</u>, was much higher in the small group. In the small group the teacher was able to guide, direct, assist, and listen more to children, and appeared to become a more significant person in the life of the child.

4. Comparisons of the <u>types of activities of children</u> in the two groups revealed few great differences. The small-group climate was observed to foster more creative, dramatic, and social experiences in the activities of block-building and playhouse. Cannon also suggested that the more noise, greater excitement, and less permissive atmosphere of the large group were less conducive to cooperative, creative play.

5. The <u>teacher's feelings and reactions to the two groups</u> were recorded in a diary. Her notes disclosed that the large group was more often described as hard, noisy, chaotic, and exhausting, while the small group was described as affectionate, relaxed, and productive and the children as more spontaneous, creative, and happy.

Elementary-School Classes

Otto and others (65) summarized the major findings of four doctoral dissertations which were completed during the 1952-53 school year and were planned as a "team" study of existing conditions and practices in 50 small and 50 large elementary-school classes. The specific purpose of this study was to ascertain what differences between the large and small classes existed in teacher load, teacher knowledge and evaluation of pupils, pupils' participation in selected classroom activities, selected techniques used in classroom teaching, building facilities, instructional aids and their frequency of use, and the scope and organization of the curriculum.

Large classes were defined as those enrolling 35 or more pupils; small classes were those enrolling 25 or fewer pupils. The median number of pupils in the large classes was 37, and the median in the small classes was 23. Thirty-four second-grade, 34 fourth-grade, and 32 sixth-grade classes were included in the study, with equal numbers of large and small classes studied at each grade level. The classes were located in 30 school systems in Texas and one in New Mexico. Data were gathered by means of a questionnaire, interviews, and observations. Nearly 500 separate items were used in the examination of elementary school programs. Analyses were made of the differences between the 50 large and 50 small classes grouped together, and also of differences between large and small classes at each grade level. Presented here are the findings for the entire group.

Of the 500 items included in the study, only 26 reflected statistically significant differences (at or beyond the 5 percent level of confidence) between the 50 large and 50 small classes. Given below is a brief discussion of some of those items on which the differences between the large and small classes were statistically significant, others where the differences approached significance, and still others which may be of interest because no significant differences were found.

Teacher load--Teacher load, designated by the term "service load," included time spent in (a) scheduled classroom duties, (b) out-of-class routine activities, (c) out-of-class professional activities, and (d) community activities. The difference between teachers of large and small classes in time spent in scheduled classroom duties was not significant. Nor were significant differences found in the hours spent in each 22 out-of-class routine activities. Differences in time spent in correcting papers, in keeping records and reports, and in giving individual help approached significance, however, with teachers of large classes spending more time at these routine activities. The total number of hours per week given to all out-of-class routine activities was significantly greater, at the 1 percent level of confidence, for teachers of large classes. Teachers of these large classes spent an estimated 18.5 hours more per week in professional activities, but the difference was not statistically significant. These first three elements of the service load, when combined, were called "the work week." A very real difference existed between the work weeks of teachers of large and small classes, with teachers of large classes spending an average of three hours more per week in these activities.

Teachers of large classes reported spending a significantly greater amount of time in community activities.

The mean service load (the four activities combined) of teachers of large classes was between four and five hours per week greater than that of teachers of small classes, a difference significant at the 1 percent level of confidence.

Teacher knowledge and evaluation of pupils-- Four areas were investigated in this section of the study.

1. Knowledge and understanding of pupils was measured by inference from teacher reports of the frequency and extent of their use of such devices and techniques as anecdotal records, interest inventories, and conferences with various related school personnel. No statistically significant differences were found between the number of teachers of small and large classes reporting use of any one, or all, of the 17 devices listed in the questionnaire. Although small numbers of teachers of both small and large classes reported use of this device, twice as many teachers of large classes as of small classes kept interest inventories on their pupils. The frequency of use of all devices was greater for teachers of large classes, but not to a significant extent.

2. Appraising and inventorying pupil progress was measured by the reported use of seven techniques and devices, such as standardized and teacher-made tests and individual pupil conferences. Differences between large and small classes in the use of five types of tests and test results and in checking written work were negligible and nonsignificant. While not significant, the difference in the extent of individual pupil conferences was very real; 50 percent of the teachers of small classes reported conferring with more than 90 percent of their class groups, while 42 percent of the teachers of large classes reported conferring with less than 30 percent of their class groups.

3. No statistically significant differences were found between the number of teachers giving help to individuals during classroom instruction and to individuals or groups of pupils outside the classroom. It was noted, however, that 28 teachers of large classes, compared with 19 teachers of small classes gave individual help outside the classroom.

4. No statistically significant differences were found between teachers of large and small classes in promoting understanding and cooperation between home and school by means of conferences or informal visits with parents at home, at school, or by telephone. Except for conferences with parents by phone, slightly greater numbers of teachers of small classes engaged in such activities.

Otto and others (65:108-109) interpreted results in this section of the study in the following way:

> The data on the use of these child study and evaluating practices and devices by

teachers of small and of large classes revealed differences so insignificant as to provide small basis for speculation. Tentatively, however, it may be suggested that teachers of small classes made more frequent use of practices involving personal contacts--anecdotal records, individual pupil conferences, individual pupil help during regular classroom instruction, and parent conferences--than did teachers of large classes. The latter apparently had greater need of devices which could be applied in group situations to gather information concerning the individual--interest inventories, individual pupil folders, diagnostic tests, written work, and group help. Teachers of large classes gave a greater amount of individual help outside regular classroom instruction than did the teachers of small classes.

Pupil participation in selected classroom activities--Teachers were asked to indicate in which of 39 selected classroom activities their pupils participated. Significant at the 1 percent level of confidence and favoring small classes was "pupils participate in making seating assignments in the classroom." Significant at the 5 percent level of confidence and favoring large classes were: "pupils handle routines connected with lunches and lunch hour"; "pupils assigned leadership roles in play and physical education activities"; and "pupils, serving in capacity of chairman, lead the group in discussion periods." Activities in which differences were large but not statistically significant were: "pupils participate in deciding what kinds of committees are needed in developing the instructional units"; and "pupils participate in planning play or physical education activities." Both were reported by more teachers of large classes than of small classes.

Classroom teaching techniques--Incorporated into an observation checklist were 255 teaching techniques, some of which might apply to several or all curriculum areas, and others which might apply only to specific subject areas. (Those subjects identified for study were arithmetic, art, health, language, physical education, reading, science, social studies, spelling, and writing.)

In only six of the 255 techniques listed as being used in these subject-matter areas were differences in usage between the 50 teachers of large classes and the 50 teachers of small classes large enough to be statistically significant at the 5 percent level of confidence. Those techniques more frequently observed in small classes were: (a) pupils in art classes are given hectographed copies to color; (b) all pupils have the same page-by-page assignments in a basal text in spelling; (c) all pupils participate in routine drill activities in spelling; and (d) teacher directs and encourages the work of individual pupils during the spelling class period. Observed more often in large classes were: (a) pupils share information by means of showing pictures in social studies; and (b) pupils in social studies participate in classroom and school management (safety patrol, student council, etc.).

Human relationship factors--In order to study the nature of the human relationships in the 100 classes, observations were made of (a) over-all tone of the emotional climate in the classroom, (b) order-maintaining techniques used by the teacher, and (c) nature of behavior exhibited by students.

1. Six possible types of classroom emotional climate, such as teacher-dominated or student-controlled, were outlined and described. No statistically significant differences in the emotional climate between large and small classes were observed.

2. A checklist of 22 most frequently used order-maintaining techniques was devised. Only eight of the 22 practices were used sufficiently by the 100 teachers to be of any consequence, and only one was used by as many as 54 of the 100 teachers. (The remaining 14 practices were used by less than 10 percent of the teachers.) Infrequent use of order-maintaining techniques was observed in equal numbers of large and small classes, and there were no statistically significant differences in the percentage of small and large classes in which any one of the 22 techniques was used. The application of such techniques appeared to be related to the self-discipline of pupils in the classroom.

Further analysis revealed that number and incidence of rule infractions were not appreciably related to mean per-pupil area, amount of seating space, or type and arrangement of seating furniture. Rule infractions did, however, appear to be related to the use of order-maintaining techniques and the nature of the classroom emotional climate.

3. Eighteen types of undesirable pupil behavior were observed; 11 were more frequent in large classes, and six in small classes. Cheating was observed with equal frequency in large and small classes. Only eight types of undesirable behavior occurred in enough classes to test the differences for statistical significance, and none was found to be significant. Approaching significance was "disturbing others by hitting, punching, etc." Exhibiting a large difference, but not approaching significance, was "promiscuous talking with others." Both types of behavior were observed more often in large classes.

Scope and organization of the curriculum--Data for this section was gathered by means of teacher-completed questionnaires, interviews, and observations. Items were grouped into

TABLE 10.--SUMMARY OF STATISTICALLY SIGNIFICANT DIFFERENCES BETWEEN PRACTICES IN 50 SMALL AND 50 LARGE ELEMENTARY-SCHOOL CLASSES

Size-Category Favored by the Difference

Small Classes	Large Classes
	Teaching Load
	Total hours per week spent in routine activities*
	Mean hours per week in teaching load as measured by Frost Formula*
	Median hours per week in teaching load as measured by Frost Formula**
	Total hours per week spent in affiliation with civic groups*
	Total hours per week spent in community activities*
	Mean and median hours per week spent in community activities*
	Mean and median hours per service week*
	Classroom Space Relationships
Mean per-pupil floor area*	Total floor area devoted to seating*
Available activity area**	
	Classroom Equipment
Prevalence of desk chairs**	Combination of two or more types of seating furniture*
	Human Relationship Factors
Pupils are discourteous to teacher or fellow pupils**	Pupils disturb others by hitting, punching, etc.*
	Pupils fight with others*
	Scope of the Curriculum
	Pupils participate in school safety patrol**
	Pupil Participation in Selected Classroom Activities
Pupils participate in making seating assignments in the classroom*	Pupils serving as chairmen lead the group or class in discussion period**
	Pupils are assigned leadership roles in play and physical education activities**
	Pupils handle routines connected with lunch hour**
	Classroom Teaching Techniques
All pupils have the same page-by-page assignment in a basal text in spelling**	Pupils share information by means of showing pictures in social studies**
All pupils in art classes are given hectographed copies to color**	Pupils participate in classroom and school management (safety patrol, student council, etc.) as part of instruction in social studies**
All pupils participate in routine drill activities in spelling**	
The teacher directs and encourages the work of individual pupils during the spelling class**	

Source:
  Otto, Henry J., and others. *Class Size Factors in Elementary Schools.* Bureau of Laboratory Schools Publication No. 4. Austin: University of Texas, 1954. p. 146-47.
    *Statistically significant at the 1 percent level of confidence.
    **Statistically significant at the 5 percent level of confidence.

eight categories. No statistically significant differences between large and small classes were found in (a) subject area offerings, (b) free time activities, (c) school and community activities, (d) homeroom activities, (e) use of dramatization, (f) special day activities, and (g) organization of the curriculum (e.g., "subject-in-isolation," "core," and "experience" curriculums). All five of the activities in the remaining category--activities related to school in general--were reported more often by teachers of large classes, but for only one (pupil participation in the school fire patrol) was the difference significant at the 5 percent level of confidence. When totals for each activity were broken down into the categories of "regularly" and "irregularly," a difference at the 1 percent level of confidence in "pupil participation in the school safety program" favored large classes.

Table 10 summarizes the 26 statistically significant differences between large and small classes found out of the nearly 500 items examined in this study. Although he concluded that the total educational programs of the large and small classes studied were not discernably different, Otto pointed out that the present study merely indicated that "small classes <u>as now taught</u> do not harbor in significant proportion their purported advantages over large classes." (65:155)

<u>Elementary classes in the More Effective Schools program</u>--Conclusions from another study emphasized, as did Otto, that where small classes existed (in this case by deliberate design), the small grouping was not used effectively. Pupil achievement, as well as other criteria, was measured in this short-term evaluation of New York City's More Effective Schools program. Although class size was only one variable in this program, some of the findings are relevant to this survey.

The More Effective Schools (MES) program, begun in 1964 in 10 elementary schools and expanded to 11 additional schools in 1965, proposes to create more effective schools by making basic changes in the areas of pupils and curriculum, personnel, school plant and organization, and community relations. Within these areas, the guiding policy calls for such specific actions as selecting participating schools to maximize the liklihood of integration, grouping classes heterogeneously, instituting team teaching, and emphasizing school-community relations. Maximum class size was set at 22 pupils. Evaluation concerned primarily comparing the quality of the in-class instructional program and its effects on participating children in ME schools with that of eight control schools, which were selected for their similarity to an ME school in terms of location and pupil population. (It should be noted that the study attempted to assess the effectiveness of implementation of the program and not to evaluate the worth of the MES concept itself.)

In October 1966, average class size in ME schools (grades 1-8) was 20.1, compared with 28.5 in control schools, 27.2 in special service schools, and 27.7 in city-wide elementary schools. At this same time, the pupil-teacher ratio (total number of pupils divided by total number of authorized teaching positions) was 12.3 in ME schools, 22.2 in control schools, 20.9 in special service schools, and 21.9 in city-wide elementary schools. It should be remembered that changes other than reduced class size were initiated in this program. No cause-effect relationship can be established between reduced class size and the evaluation findings.

Positive results were found in the areas of teacher morale and attitude, over-all school climate, and parent and community attitude. According to the observers, the atmosphere and climate in most of the ME schools was characterized by "enthusiasm, interest, and hope, and a belief among all levels of staff that they were in a setting in which they could function." The parents and community also responded "with interest and enthusiasm to the MES program in their neighborhood schools." (21:120-21)

The data also indicated, however, that

the MES program has made no significant difference in the functioning of children, whether this was measured by observers rating what children did in class, and how they do it, or whether it was measured by children's ability in mathematics or reading on standardized tests. The data . . . show that children in classes in ME schools were not behaving any differently than children in classes in the . . . control schools or in classes in other special service schools.

. . . .

We see in these data no reason to expect better achievement in reading or arithmetic from the MES program as now constituted, nor any reason to believe that the program will result in significant alteration in the pattern of increasing retardation as a child progresses through the grades (21:121-22)

Observations of the MES classrooms revealed lack of adaptation of the instructional program to the small classes; less than half (45 percent) of the observers' ratings indicated that the small class situation was being used effectively, while 55 percent of the ratings indicated ineffective use of small classes. (21:88)

A majority of the lessons observed "could have been taught to larger classes with no loss in effectiveness."

Fox concluded that administrative changes, such as smaller classes, reduced pupil-teacher ratio, and specialized teaching, psychological, social, and health services "will have a dramatic impact on the attitudes and perceptions of the adults who function in, or observe that school." He also concluded, however, that although these administrative changes are "elaborate and expensive in terms of both money and professional time, [they] will not, in and of themselves, result in improvement in children's functioning." (21:122-23)

First-grade reading achievement--In 1961, Frymier (22) reported a study to measure the effect of class size on the reading achievement of first-grade pupils. Subjects were pupils on whom complete achievement data were available in six large (more than 36 pupils) and nine small (fewer than 30 pupils) first-grade classes. A total of 201 pupils (101 boys, 100 girls) in large classes and 219 pupils (111 boys, 108 girls) in small classes was studied. Frymier reported that for all practical purposes the two groups were similar in terms of visual and auditory acuity and physical health. Pupils in small classes were slightly older than pupils in large classes (mean age of 81.0 months compared with 79.1 months). Readiness tests administered at the beginning of first grade showed pupils in large classes to be significantly above pupils in small classes at the 1 percent level of confidence. There were some slight, "but probably insignificant," differences between the two groups of teachers. All teachers had B.S. degrees, but one teacher of a small class had a M.S. degree. The teachers of large classes appeared to be slightly more experienced.

Achievement was measured by (a) reading achievement test scores at the end of the year, (b) mean grade placement, and (c) retention and promotion rates. On the Williams Primary Reading Achievement Test, large-class pupils had a mean raw score of 19.21, and small-class pupils had a mean raw score of 22.58, a difference significant at the .001 level of confidence. Pupils in large classes had a mean grade placement of 1.62 years at the end of the year, compared with 1.75 years for small-class pupils. The difference between retention rates for large classes (23 percent were retained) and small classes (17 percent were retained) was not significant.

Frymier concluded that there was "clear evidence . . . that class size influenced achievement in reading for these first grade students." (22:93)

Junior High-School Classes

Pupil achievement--Menniti (37) made a statistical study of the relationship between class size and pupil achievement in the eighth-grade classes in the Catholic dioceses of Harrisburg (Pa.) and Evansville (Ind.). In this status study, Menniti compared achievement test raw scores and IQ scores of pairs of classes--small classes having 35 or fewer pupils and large classes having 40 or more pupils. (Members of the classes were also grouped according to ability levels.) Eliminated on the basis of supervisory reports were overcrowded classes, classes with inferior physical conditions, and classes with teachers of superior or inferior ratings.

Analysis of data showed:

1. There was a significant difference in achievement in mathematics in large classes for the average-ability pupils of both dioceses.

2. Significant differences in reading achievement of average pupils were found in the large classes in the Harrisburg diocese.

3. The achievement of low IQ groups was affected in both reading and mathematics, but not as much as the average pupils.

4. The achievement of upper-IQ groups showed no significant differences in large classes.

Team teaching in various-sized classes-- Goldstein (23) referred to a four-week summer institute in team teaching which experimented with classes of various sizes. Junior high-school pupils attending the summer session for an "enriched academic program" were organized into regular classes, seminar groups, and large classes. Specific class enrollments were not reported, but Goldstein had previously referred to regular classes of "30 or so" and large classes of perhaps "90 or more." At the end of the summer session, pupils were asked, "In which sized class did you learn the most, and in which did you learn the least?" Approximately 250 pupils gave usable replies, and their responses, which are shown below, indicated that the majority felt they "learned the most" in seminar groups and "learned the least" in large classes.

	Learned the most	Learned the least
Regular classes	37.8%	13.1%
Seminar groups	54.6	29.0
Large groups	7.6	57.9

High-School Classes

Algebra achievement--Anderson and others (4) in 1963 reported a study in which subjects were 120 pupils who scored at or above the 90th percentile on the Differential Aptitude Numerical Text. They were randomly placed in two one-semester accelerated algebra classes--one large class of 80 pupils and one small class of 40 pupils. One instructor taught both classes, with the assistance of two 12th-grade aides, but taught no other classes. Analysis of results of scores from the Sequential Test of Educational Progress revealed no statistically significant differences in achievement between the two classes.

Chemistry grades--Anderson (5) compared final examination grades in chemistry of pupils from 73 selected high schools in nine states. When classes were equated on the basis of intelligence and knowledge of subject, Anderson found that pupils in small classes made higher final examination grades than pupils in large classes.

General mathematics achievement--Madden (36) sought to determine if there were any significant differences in achievement of pupils when they were taught ninth-grade general mathematics in large (70-85 pupils) or regular (25-40 pupils) groups. Pupils were pre-tested during the second week and post-tested during the final week of the fall semester on separate forms of a standardized mathematics test. For purposes of subgroup analysis, scores from a quantitative thinking ability test were used to place pupils at three ability levels.

Pre-tests showed the groups to be statistically equivalent at the beginning of the course. Post-test results showed the achievement of the pupils in the large group to be significantly above (at the 5 percent level of confidence) that of the regular group pupils. Pupils of average ability achieved significantly higher (at the 5 percent level) in the large group than in the regular group.

Generally, there was no significant interaction among the several combinations of method (large vs. regular group), ability level, or sex.

English, geometry, American history, and biology achievement--Johnson and Lobb (30) reported on the first phase of a three-year study in Jefferson County, Colorado, the purpose of which was "to investigate promising ways of improving instruction and utilizing the staff in the secondary schools." This first phase, which took place during the 1957-58 school year, was designed to determine the effects of class size upon achievement, attitudes, and behavior of learners. Subjects in the study were 1,075 tenth- and eleventh-grade pupils in eight high schools. Classes of 10, 20, 35, 60, and 70 pupils were specifically organized in the courses of English III, plane geometry, American history, and biology. In order more nearly to equate teacher load, each class of 60 and 70 had two teachers. Of the 35 participating teachers, 26 entered the experiment voluntarily. Pupils were randomly selected for the classes, except that those pupils in the classes of 10 were chosen, on the basis of intelligence, achievement, and teacher judgment, as those most likely to profit from small-group instruction.

Pupils were pre-tested by a test of mental ability and tests of educational development, which were given at the beginning of the year, and post-tested by achievement tests. In addition, each teacher submitted a weekly report on class activities, which were classified as "persistently traditional," "occasionally traditional," or "persistently experimental."

The researchers concluded that size of class in itself produced no significant differences in the criteria. There were no significant differences in pupil achievement. Small groups of high capacity learners were neither academically nor economically feasible. Students had not been harmed by participating in large group work. According to Johnson and Lobb, groups of all sizes were equally effective--for entirely different learning situations.

Studies of Class Size in Other Countries

Important questions relating to class size have been studied in several countries; Clark (14) summarized briefly such class size research.

He reported that in England and Wales a sample of 4,000 eight-year-old pupils was tested on mechanical reading ability and intelligence. There were apparently no significant differences between the average performances of pupils in classes of varying sizes.

A study of a sample of 7,000 seven- to 11-year-old pupils in 51 primary schools in Kent "found good reading ability to be significantly associated with large schools, superior buildings, urban areas, and large classes."

A study in Scotland of 76,000 10-year-old pupils revealed little relationship between class size and median scores in English comprehension.

A study in Western Australia of fifth- and seventh-grade pupils was directed more particularly at the effects of retardation and acceleration on reading and arithmetic, but produced some data relevant to class size. For both subjects and both grade levels, the general order of performance, in descending order, was in classes of (a) 50 or more pupils, (b) 30-39 pupils, (c) 40-49 pupils, and (d) fewer than 30 pupils.

Clarke and Richel (15) reported a comparative analysis of class size and other factors in public school systems in two Alberta (Canada) cities of over 200,000 population. Both systems were under the authority of the provincial government; therefore, the systems had similar school organizations, the same source of teacher certification, and the same curriculum. Other factors known or thought to affect school achievement (e.g., socioeconomic background) were thought to be similar in the cities. Yet pupils in one city (city-AB) consistently scored higher, over a four-year period, than did pupils in the other city (city-CD) on a set of external examinations given at the end of grade 9 by the provincial Department of Education, which controlled the setting, marked the examinations, etc.

Attempting to determine the cause(s) of this difference, Clarke and Richel compared the two cities' systems on the factors of (a) scholastic aptitude of pupils; (b) quality of teaching, as measured by supervision, teacher education, and experience; (c) length of time students are learning, as measured by student transiency and attendance; (d) class size over the nine years of learning; and (e) promotion practices in earlier grades (i.e., selective versus continuous promotion). Records of pupils in the ninth grade during the academic years 1957-58 through 1960-61 were used.

For the majority of their first nine years of schooling, city-CD pupils had experienced classes which were considerably larger than those of city-AB pupils. Class-by-class comparisons were possible in 85 instances. Of these, the mean class size in city-CD exceeded that of city-AB in 72 instances, and in 53 instances the mean class size in city-CD was considerably larger than the city-AB mean class size (i.e., the city-CD mean class size was one-or-more-pupils greater than the city-AB mean class size in the comparable class level and year). Class size in both cities had decreased from the first-grade enrollment in the early 1950's to the ninth-grade enrollment eight years later, but the decrease was greater in city-AB. In recent years, class size at the junior high-school level was typically three students more in city-CD than in city-AB.

Data from analysis of the other factors led Clarke and Richel to conclude that "a combination of smaller classes and better qualified teachers produces better results on Grade 9 examinations, or conversely, that larger classes and more poorly qualified teachers produces poorer results on the Grade 9 examinations." (15:71)

Haskell (26) studied pupil attitudes and attainment in two small and two large geometric drawing classes in an English secondary school. The large classes enrolled 34 and 35 pupils; the small classes, 17 pupils each. One class of each size was socially organized according to the pupils' own choices, while the other two classes were non-sociometric. Held constant were the factors of pupil intelligence, pre-test knowledge, sex and age, instructor differences, and classroom and equipment facilities. Attainment and attitude tests were given at the end of each of the first three terms. Haskell found no significant differences in attainment between the large and small classes, with the exception of third-term scores, which showed a difference significant at the 5 percent level of confidence. There was no evidence that class size affected attitudes. It appeared that socially organized classes (i.e., classes organized according to the pupils' own choices) favorably affected the pupils' attitudes, but did not affect pupil attainment.

Junior College and College Classes

Although not of primary purpose in this summary, a few studies of class size at the junior college and university level are of interest.

<u>Junior college English achievement</u>--Hopper and Keller (28) reported a study of large and small classes of a one-semester English course, the purpose of which was to teach students how to write "clear, concise, meaningful, stimulating, and fully developed prose." The subjects, 274 junior-college freshmen who had earned high-school English grades of C or better, were randomly divided into three sections of 56 students each, and four sections of 28 students each. Teacher A had two sections of 28 and one of 56 students, and Teachers B and C each had one large and one small section. The instructors used the same teaching methods in large and small classes. Prior to the investigation, two of the instructors were "extremely skeptical" about the effectiveness of large classes, but the third professed an open mind. Achievement was measured by means of pre- and post-tests, both of which included a writing sample and an essay analysis. Papers were graded anonymously by predetermined departmental scoring standards.

The conclusion from this study was that, on the basis of the one measure of net improvement, the variable of class size was not important, when there was a difference of 28 students between small and large classes. In all sections of small and large classes taught by all three teachers, students showed much improvement, but the differences in net change between paired large and small classes were not significant.

Evaluation forms completed by the students at the end of the semester revealed no significant preference for small classes over large <u>per se</u>, but there were individual problems that seemed to stem from class size. For example, students in Teacher A's large classes complained of "buzzing in the back of the room," while students in his small classes did not. With more than chance occurrence, students of Teacher B indicated preference for small classes, arguing that in small classes there was greater opportunity for individual attention and less feeling of shyness. In contrast, students of Teacher C indicated more than chance preference for large classes, commenting that large classes are more stimulating because of the greater variety of student responses. (It was noted that prior teacher evaluations had suggested that Teacher C would do well in a large group.)

College American Government achievement and attitudes--Rohrer (66) reported a study of large and small classes in a beginning course which introduced students to the general principles and processes in American Government. The two experimental variables were class size and the lecture versus the discussion methods of presentation. (The variables of student age, sex, measured academic aptitude and initial mastery of American Government, veteran/nonveteran status, and college classification, as well as the subject matter were equated, controlled, or confounded.) Instructors A and B each taught one large section (332 and 309 students) and one small section (31 and 34 students). Instructor C taught two small sections (27 and 24 students)--one by the lecture method and one by the discussion method. Each student was placed in a class according to which one would best fit into his schedule, but pretests indicated essentially even distribution of student aptitude and prior knowledge of the subject.

The instructors made identical assignments, used the same textbooks, etc., and none had prior knowledge of student achievement or attitudes. The students were informed that final grades would depend solely on departmental examinations.

The two criteria in the study were (a) measured attitudes of the students toward the difficulty of the course material and their interest in it, and (b) the measured achievement of the students.

Results of post-tests of achievement in American government revealed no statistically significant differences in mean gains of large and small classes.

The students' attitudes toward the difficulty of the course were significantly related to both the teacher and the size of class, and these two variables interacted. Rohrer concluded that the attitude of the instructor toward the size of class in which he was teaching and his skills in handling large and small sections were the important variables operating in this experiment. The students' expressed interest in the subject matter also varied significantly with the instructor and the size of class, and once again these two variables interacted. No significant differences were observed between the small classes taught by the lecture and the discussion methods.

Rohrer suggested that his most significant finding was that amount of achievement and students' attitudes varied as a function of the course instructor, and did not vary as a function of class size.

Social science performance--Cammarosano and Santopolo (12) reported a study of Fordham College during the 1956-57 academic year to measure the effects of large and small classes on "desirable student performance." A large section (60 students) and a small section (30 students) were organized for each of three two-semester courses: freshman-level Principles of Economics; sophomore-level Introduction to American Government; and sophomore-level Introductory Sociology. Each pair of sections was taught by the same instructor, who used the same syllabus and the same method of teaching--a combination of lecture, question, and discussion techniques--for both sections. Participating in the experiment were instructors who had been recognized for their experience, dynamism, and lively classroom manner. Graduate assistants handled noninstructional business for both sections. Participating students were selected on the basis of their high school or freshman academic ratings, and all were of middle range ability (high-C/low-B) students. Pairs of sections were equated first on these academic ratings, and later on CEEB scores.

Three criteria were used to measure "desirable student performance":

1. Command of academic subject matter was measured by first- and second-semester grades, which were based on quizzes, examinations, and written assignments. Class mean semester grade averages showed significant differences between large and small sections of none of the courses, for neither semester.

2. Social awareness, i.e., interest in public events which affect society's well being, was measured by a specially designed unannounced test. Class means on this test showed no significant differences, when large- and small-section means were compared by course.

3. Principled synthesis of social outlook, i.e., control of scientific and philosophical principles in appraising public issues, was measured by three specially designed, unannounced tests, one for each course. Only large- and small-section sociology class means differed at

the 5 percent level of confidence, with the small-class mean greater. Sections of the other two courses did not differ significantly.

Thus, on only one of the 12 measures did the large and small sections differ significantly. Of the other 11 measures, the small sections were superior on five, the large sections on five, and the sections were equal on one.

During the first semester, students were asked for their reactions toward the large classes. The large sections appeared as satisfied as the small in opportunity for discussion and questions. Thought justifiable by the authors were the large-section students' complaints about physical crowding.

Participating teachers were conscious of a greater effort to establish informality in large classes, to assure distribution of discussion, and to enlist participation of disinclined class members. The instructors' principal criticism--that the use of graduate assistants diluted the intimacy of the professor-student contact made it difficult to uncover individual problems, etc.--applied equally to large and small sections. Rough calculations showed a saving, through use of the large sections, of about 25 percent of the instructor's time, primarily in the areas of class time and paper grading.

Future Class Size Research

It has already been suggested that in the future researchers will need to deal with the many questions related to class size in a multi-dimensional fashion. At least two other recent developments may also influence future research--preschool education and Head Start programs. In recent years there has been great interest in the education of preschool children, particularly those children whose disadvantaged backgrounds have hindered their later socio-educational-cultural development. The desire to overcome these handicaps suggested the need for intensely individualized attention to each child. As a result, the federally financed Head Start programs have set as their goal two adult aides to every trained teacher for a class of 15 children.

An NEA Research Division survey estimated the pupil-teacher ratio for full-year (1966-67) and summer (1966) Head Start programs operated by public school systems with enrollments of 300 or more. (52) The findings are given below. For both half-day programs and other programs, for both summer and full-year programs, the ratio reflects the fact that many teachers are responsible for more than one class daily.

	Estimated total number of pupils	Estimated total number of teachers	Ratio
Summer program, 1966			
Full day	46,591	2,995	15.6
Half day	233,842	11,494	20.3[a]
Other	11,999	655	18.3[a]
Full-year program, 1966-67			
Full day	11,457	735	15.6
Half day	37,538	1,444	30.0[a]
Other	8,013	395	20.3[a]

[a] This ratio reflects the fact that many of the teachers were responsible for more than one class daily.

Many people have acclaimed the Head Start program a success, and most have attributed at least part of its success to the reduced pupil-teacher ratio, e.g., a professor of education at San Francisco State College (31:33). A member of the Public Affairs staff of the Office of Economic Opportunity asserted that Head Start results have "validated the assumption" that more smaller classes would solve many preprimary and primary school problems. He cited program results which consistently indicate that the adult-child ratio of 3:15 had tremendous effect on the children's growth. One eight-week program produced an eight-to-ten point gain in children's IQ's. Another produced an average 14 months' growth on a picture-vocabulary test of word recognition. Results of still another program showed such gains that by first grade, participating low-income children matched their middle-income classmates in reading readiness. (20)

These testimonials undoubtedly are not representative of all Head Start programs, and no attempt was made to survey the project results. The fact that some of these preschool programs did produce positive results, however, may be relevant to the questions of class size in the primary grades.

Variable class sizes and flexible scheduling-- Operating on the assumption that the size of class should be appropriate to the teaching method used, the purpose of the meeting, and the type of learning desired, educators have suggested several versions of a variable class-size plan for the secondary school. For example, the National Association of Secondary-School Principals has recommended large-group instruction (involving 100 or more pupils), small-group discussion (12-15 pupils), and individual study (1-3 pupils). (77)

Sidney Besvinick (8) described five different class sizes.

1. Classes of <u>unlimited size</u> would enable efficient "one-way transmission" of knowledge, information, and opinion by instructors and guest speakers. Class discussion or question-answer sessions would not be attempted.

2. The purpose of classes of <u>moderate size</u> (40-50 pupils) would be skill development (e.g., mathematics, physical education, typing). The teacher would supervise individuals, but would not attempt to communicate with the class as a whole.

3. Classes of <u>activity size</u> (25 pupils) would be appropriate for science or language laboratories, art classes, or vocational shops.

4. Discussion, clarification, and exploration would take place in <u>small groups</u> of 10-12 pupils.

5. Provisions for <u>independent study</u> would involve assigning pupils to central "subject-matter stations," where they would work on material of their choice but related to that station's emphasis. As a student showed proficiency in a certain area, he would be released from reporting to the teacher and would then be free to concentrate his attention wherever he wished. The student would gradually be allowed more freedom of action, as he was able to use the latitude given him.

Accompanying experimentation with varied class size has been the use of flexible scheduling, which is based on the assumption that the nature of the subject should dictate not only the size of the class, but also the length of the scheduled period. Hamilton and Madgic (24) and Beggs (7), among others, have reported implementation of flexible scheduling and variable class size in secondary schools.

Experimentation with these arrangements, as well as with team teaching and other means of staff utilization, will undoubtedly influence class size research in the future.

Recommendations and Standards

Recommendations for class size, teacher load, and/or numerical staffing adequacy are abundant. It appears, however, that flexibility, rather than rigid adherence to predetermined standards, is being emphasized more often. This section contains illustrative excerpts from official statements of national education organizations that have made recent recommendations relating to class size. Also included are the standards set by several of the regional agencies which accredit secondary schools. The most recent date when the recommendation was made, the resolution was adopted or reaffirmed, etc., precedes the reference number of the document. For all groups, the most recent statement which could be located has been used. In some cases, a change in policy over the past several years has been noted.

National Education Association

The platform of the National Education Association recommends:

    a. A minimum of 50 professional staff members per 1,000 pupils in a school system.

    b. Reasonable, carefully defined work-loads, including time for planning and a limit to the noninstructional tasks required of teachers.

    c. Class size permitting appropriate individual attention for every pupil; no basic learnings class in elementary school to exceed 25 pupils per teacher. (1967; 40:65)

Educational Policies Commission NEA-AASA

The Educational Policies Commission, which was sponsored jointly by the NEA and the American Association of School Administrators, made the following comments on class size:

The primary consideration affecting class size is the individual need of each pupil for professional assistance. Class size may properly vary with the subject taught, the characteristics of the student body, and the number of professional personnel available to supplement the teacher's efforts in guiding pupils.

The results of research on class size support the common view of teachers: that for most learning situations small classes provide a better opportunity for education than large ones. The research does not point to any invariable optimum size. It indicates rather that as class size increases, the teacher finds it more difficult to perform his varied roles and, especially in the areas requiring individual attention, his effectiveness diminishes.

Some learning situations [as when the role of the pupil is primarily to observe or to listen] are suitable for large numbers....

Where the pupil's performance is to be observed, evaluated, and criticized by a qualified teacher, the importance of limited numbers is self-evident.

....

A teacher skilled in providing the type of personal attention needed by elementary pupils is unlikely to be able to supply it continuously in classes of more than twenty-five.

....

Because desirable class sizes vary so widely, staff size may be more important than class size.

....

In any school system there should be enough competent professionals to ensure that every pupil receives needed attention. Where this standard is met, classes are of various sizes, depending on subjects taught and the characteristics of the student body. If the school program is to provide wide opportunities, and if the supplementary services of guidance counselors, librarians, coordinators, and administrators are to be available, there is obviously some minimum staff size below which needed professional services cannot be supplied. Experience in good school systems indicates that this minimum is about fifty professionals per thousand pupils....

It should be emphasized that this ratio is a minimum. Better services to pupils, and consequently higher quality education, can be provided with a competent staff of larger size. In communities where schools are best supported, staffs range up to seventy professionals per thousand pupils. (1959; 57:14-17)

Looking at some Contemporary Issues in American Education, the Commission commented:

While no precise ideal class size can be established, it is clear that as the number of children increases, the possibility of individualizing instruction diminishes.

Pending a time when research yields more conclusive answers, the experience of competent persons who work in and know elementary schools should be heeded. Such persons seem to agree that the opportunity to adapt programs to individuals diminishes rapidly as classes exceed 25 pupils. The ability to provide needed services to pupils, of course, varies with the needs of those pupils and the ability of the teacher to perceive those needs. Thus classes of 25 might be organized in which no teacher could possible serve all the children because of the great variations in needs or the inclusion of pupils with particularly difficult problems of personal adjustment. These problems require outside services. Thus the key concept is staff size rather than class size. (1960; 55:22-23)

Regarding the education of the disadvantaged American, the Commission stated:

One thing . . . seems certain: every child should have the attention of a skilled and understanding teacher. This need is especially marked in the case of disadvantaged children because their background prepares them poorly for formal education. When experimental programs for educating these children have seemed to give evidence of best progress, they have incorporated smaller-than-normal classes. Although classes of twenty-five children have long been taken by most professionals as a goal for children whose home background is favorable, it appears that classes of twenty--or even fewer--are better for disadvantaged pupils. (1962; 56:20-21)

NEA Office of Professional Development and Welfare

The Office of Professional Development and Welfare of the NEA has published a book entitled Profiles of Excellence. One of the many criteria recommended for evaluating the quality of a school system is the number of professional personnel per 1,000 pupils. Suggested standards for judging inferior and superior school systems are as follows:

Inferior: There are fewer than 35 professional personnel per 1,000 pupils, and little attention is given to the most effective deployment of staff.

Superior: There are at least 65 professional personnel per 1,000 pupils. Continuous attention is given to the deployment of the professional staff in the most effective manner possible, taking into account the various geographical and social factors prevalent in the district. Professional personnel other than classroom teachers account for at least 15 of the 65 professional personnel per 1,000 pupils. (1966; 48:17)

Association of Classroom Teachers, NEA

The Platform of the Department of Classroom Teachers of the NEA (the name of which was officially changed in 1967 to the Association of Classroom Teachers) states:

Teacher Load:

The Department believes that a major part of the teachers of the nation are carrying a professional load too heavy for the greatest service to children and to the community. It believes that teachers should be freed from excessive clerical work, that there should be maintained a teacher-pupil ratio of 1 to 25 based upon persons actually engaged in classroom teaching and the total student enrollment, that class size should not exceed 30 students per teacher, and that school-day schedules should provide adequate time for lesson planning and pupil counseling. (1962; 41:69)

Department of Elementary School Principals, NEA

Until recently the Department of Elementary School Principals' (NEA) resolution on class size and quality of education stated, in part:

> Experience indicates that a teacher is unlikely to be able to observe, evaluate, and instruct each pupil continuously and successfully when the class has more than twenty-five students. (1963; 45:37)

This resolution further stated that

> the Department favors the assignment of at least fifty professional personnel to each one thousand students.

At its 1966 business meeting, however, the Department adopted the following new resolution on class and school size:

> For years, many educators have believed that there is an optimum size for the elementary school and for individual classes. A number of recent developments—for example, improvements in school plant design, changing patterns of staff utilization, and major modifications in curriculum—provide alternatives which necessitate serious reconsideration of an inflexible position.
>
> The Department of Elementary School Principals, NEA, therefore wishes to encourage educators to question the assumption that there is any one ideal class or school size. In making this recommendation, the Department emphasizes the continuing importance of maintaining an appropriate number of professionally qualified teachers in relation to the number of pupils in the school. It further emphasizes that whatever the school and class size, the organizational pattern must help teachers to identify and understand each child's needs, interests, and abilities and to mobilize the total resources of the school in directing his learning and development. (1966; 46:66)

National Association of Secondary-School Principals, NEA

The Commission on the Experimental Study of the Utilization of Staff in the Secondary School, appointed by the National Association of Secondary-School Principals, believes that the size and nature of instruction groups should vary with the purposes to be achieved and the content to be learned. The Commission sees the following grouping for instruction in the secondary school of the future:

> The secondary school of the future will not have standard classes of 25 to 35 students meeting five days a week on inflexible schedules. Both the size of the groups and the length of the classes will vary from day to day. Methods of teaching, student groupings, and teacher and pupil activities will adjust to the purposes and content of instruction.

The Commission sees the schools organized around three kinds of activities: large-group instruction, individual study, and small-group discussion.

> Large group instruction will include a number of activities carried out in groups of 100 or more students.
>
> The activities undertaken before these large groups are introduction, motivation, explanation, exploration, planning, group study, enrichment, generalization, and evaluation. These large-group activities will occupy about 40 percent of the students' time.
>
> Students will engage in <u>study</u> activities as individuals, or in groups of two or three, with a minimum of constant supervision. Teachers and other staff personnel will serve more as consultants than task masters. Conferences between students and instructors will be held whenever necessary to clarify goals, content, and personal problems. Students will read, listen to records and tapes, view, question, experiment, examine, consider evidence, analyze, investigate, think, write, create, memorize, record, make, visit, and self-appraise. These activities will take place in project and materials centers, museums, workshops, libraries, and laboratories, in and outside the school.

The Commission states that the amount of time for individual study will vary according to subject and student maturity but that on an average it will total about 40 percent of the students' time.

> Small groups of 12 to 15 students and a teacher will pit mind against mind to sharpen understanding. They will examine terms and concepts, solve problems, and reach areas of agreement and disagreement. At the same time they will learn about getting along together. This is primarily a student activity with the teacher sitting in as counselor, consultant, and evaluator. The <u>discussion</u> activities will occupy about 20 percent of the students' time. (1959; 77:7-11)

American Association of School Administrators, NEA

The Platform of the American Association of School Administrators, which was adopted in 1951 and remained unchanged until 1967, stated in part that "we as school administrators propose to work for...smaller classes, more attention to each individual, and more adequate materials and equipment--thus providing a better educational program for each child." (1966; 1:240) The Platform of AASA as revised and adopted in 1967 contains no specific mention of class size. (1967; 2:191-93)

A publication of the AASA Commission on School Buildings, Schools for America, states that "the need for grouping children in groups of varying sizes has been more clearly recognized" in recent years, and the key phrases in school building have become "flexibility," "fluidity," and "variability of space." (1967; 3:23-24)

This same publication does suggest that in early childhood education--for preschool children three to five years old--"class groups should be limited to 15 children." It continues: "The regular staff should number at least one for five children or three for each class group of fifteen. At least one of the three should be experienced and trained." (1967; 3:89)

Association for Supervisory and Curriculum Development, NEA

The 1963 Resolution of the Association for Supervision and Curriculum Development read:

WHEREAS, certain forces have been exerting pressure for a mass approach to education; and

WHEREAS, the present state of knowledge based on research in learning and class size would indicate that small instructional groups are important in obtaining particular types of learning; and

WHEREAS, a requisite for effective instruction in a group of any size is qualified professional personnel in sufficient quantity that a student can receive personal attention at critical junctures in the learning process; therefore,

BE IT RESOLVED, that the Association for Supervision and Curriculum Development go on record in support of 60-70 professionals per 1,000 pupils and that in the total professional personnel the proportion of classroom teachers should be at least one for every 25 pupils; and

BE IT FURTHER RESOLVED, that the Association for Supervision and Curriculum Development urge that a suitable research framework which attempts to define and measure a broad variety of skills, attitudes, and understanding be used in any experimentation with class size. (1963; 6:15)

NEA Project on the Instructional Program of the Public Schools

The NEA Project on Instruction, in its publication, Education in a Changing Society, identified the task of organizing of the school and the classroom as one of the broad decision areas in developing instructional programs. Within this broad area, the Project made the following recommendations for classroom size:

In order to provide individually planned programs for learners, taking into account the specific objectives to be achieved, the horizontal organization of the school should permit flexibility in assigning pupils to instructional groups that may range in size from one pupil to as many as a hundred or more. Well-planned cooperative efforts among teachers--efforts such as team teaching, for example--should be encouraged and tested. (1963; 39:141)

The Project further recommended that:

In schools where the classroom is the unit of organization, teachers should organize learners frequently into smaller groups of varying types and sizes. Decisions as to size and membership of such groups should be based on knowledge about learners and on the specific educational purposes to be served at a given time for each learner. (1963; 39:142)

Department of Elementary-Kindergarten-Nursery Education, NEA

At its 1964 annual meeting, the Department of Elementary-Kindergarten-Nursery Education, NEA, reaffirmed its 1963 resolution on class size, which read:

We urge the officers and membership of the DEKNE to support and work to achieve a ratio not to exceed 25 children per teacher per classroom in the elementary school-day in grades 1-6. The number of children assigned to a single session of Kindergarten, housed in one room, shall not exceed 20. (1963 and 1964; 43)

Resolutions adopted by DEKNE at its 1965 meeting contained no specific recommendation about class size, but the Department did adopt a resolution concerning the Economic Opportunity Act, which read in part:

BE IT RESOLVED, that the Department of Elementary-Kindergarten-Nursery Education of the National Education Association exert effort toward the establishment and maintenance of high standards of these programs [OEO-financed educational programs for special groups of young children] to insure that:

....

7. Size of groups allow for intimate relationships between pupil, teacher, and parent. (1965; 44)

The resolution on early childhood services adopted at the 1966 meeting of the DEKNE contained no reference to class size. (1966; 42)

National Commission on Teacher Education and Professional Standards, NEA

The National Commission on Teacher Education and Professional Standards of the NEA has recommended the following standards:

Class size should be determined by the size of the groups in which the teacher can give individual guidance and in which children, in various stages of development, can live effectively. The situation should enable a teacher to know each child individually, to be familiar with his home, his problems, his aspirations, and his possibilities, and to counsel with him according to his needs.

The following maximum enrollments for each teacher are recommended:

Special classes for exceptional children: 15.

Kindergarten and first grade: 20. (Forty pupils in kindergarten if different children attend morning and afternoon sessions.)

Other classes in elementary and secondary schools: 25.

Total pupil-hours for a teacher in a departmentalized secondary situation: 100. (It is recommended that elementary schools and special-subject areas require adjustment of these figures.) (1959; 47:61)

Association for Childhood Education International

Alice V. Keliher presented the position of the Association for Childhood Education International:

Experience tells us that 25 in an elementary classroom is a desirable maximum. Where difficult conditions prevail, as with the disadvantaged Head Start children, a ratio of 5 to one adult with 15 in a single group has produced fine results. We seem to have arrived at a consensus that retarded and handicapped children should be in classes of 10 to 15.6/

This agreement as to the need for small classes for handicapped children prevails because it is clear at the outset that these children need individual attention. "But," Keliher continued in the next paragraph, "why should not individual attention be given to all children?" (1966; 31:5)

Standards Set by Regional Accrediting Agencies

The <u>North Central Association of College and Secondary Schools</u> has set the following standards for secondary schools:

The ratio of pupils to teachers and other professional staff members of the high school shall not exceed 27 to 1. Only a staff member's time actually devoted to duties in the high school may be counted in determining the pupil-teacher ratio. (1966; 61:154)

The Commission on Secondary Schools of the <u>Northwest Association of Secondary and Higher Schools</u> has set the following standards:

The Association requires that no school should show excessive teacher load. This <u>shall</u> be interpreted to mean that:

1. The enrollment of students as shown in the Annual Report divided by the full-time equivalency of the professional staff members <u>shall</u> give a quotient not greater than 25. The student-teacher ratio is to be determined by dividing the total enrollment of students by the full-time equivalency of professional staff members for such time as they give to high school work and management. (1962; 62:14)

The Northwest Association standards also state that:

In order to secure optimum benefits in secondary education, it is recommended that the individual class size should not exceed thirty students except where the content and/or methods of instruction permit effective work with larger groups. (1962; 62:15)

The <u>Southern Association of Colleges and Schools</u> has set the following standard for class size in elementary schools:

6/ "Effective Learning and Teacher-Pupil Ratio," by Alice V. Keliher. From CHILDHOOD EDUCATION, September 1966, Vol. 43, No. 1. By permission of the author and the Association for Childhood Education International, 3615 Wisconsin Avenue, N.W., Washington, D.C. 20016.

Membership in all elementary classes shall average thirty pupils or less, and in no case shall exceed a maximum of thirty-five pupils in any class. (1966; 73:262)

The Joint Study Committee of the commissions on Secondary Schools and on Research and Service, Southern Association, assumed a maximum junior high-school class size of 30 pupils in average daily membership when they studied the organization and administration of the high school. (1958; 74:75)

The Southern Association's Commission on Secondary Schools has set the following standards for secondary schools:

Sufficient professional staff shall be assigned to a school to provide a maximum pupil-professional staff ratio of 22-1. Seven hundred and fifty (750) are the currently acceptable maximum pupil periods per week. Justification of academic classes in excess of 35 must be reported to the State Committee in writing. (1967; 73:126)

The Commission on Secondary Schools of the Middle States Association of Colleges and Secondary Schools has recommended simply, "The [school] staff should be adequate in number and adequately paid." (1965; 38:2)

School Board and Administrative Policy on Class Size and Teacher-Pupil Ratio

Written Policies on Class Size

The Educational Research Service, a joint service of the NEA Research Division and the American Association of School Administrators, included in a 1967 survey of large school systems a question asking whether the school board had adopted any "formal recommendations regarding size of class." (54) Thirty-six of the 128 responding systems answered this question affirmatively, and 22 returned copies of their current written policy. Some of the recommendations were formal, board-approved policies, while others were administrative guidelines or regulations.

The specifications for class size varied. Some gave minimum and maximum figures, while others set only maximums, and still others used average class size as the guide. Teacher-pupil ratio and over-all teacher load also were often used.

Many of the policies made special provisions for class size in atypical situations. Among these were a formula for determining class size when teacher aides were utilized, class size for combination-grade classes, and class sizes for schools of varying enrollments.

The following statements are illustrative segments (in some cases paraphrased) of formal recommendations regarding class size which were reported to the Educational Research Service and appeared in the circular cited above. (54:19-24)

1. (Administrative policy) In the senior high and six-year [high] schools, the teaching staff shall be determined by dividing the total daily pupil periods by 140. In the junior high schools, the total pupil periods shall be divided by 155. In junior high schools located in areas of high population density and mobility, the total pupil periods shall be divided by 150.

    In regular graded classes the pupil-teacher ratio will range from 33 to 36. "A teacher will be added when at the beginning of a semester the average class size exceeds 36, and may be withdrawn if the average class size is less than 33." In areas of high population density and mobility, classes shall be organized on a pupil-teacher ratio of 29 to 32 pupils per teacher.

    Classes for the deaf and blind shall enroll not fewer than 5 and not more than 10 pupils. Special adjustment classes shall enroll not fewer than 15 nor more than 25 pupils. Classes for the educable mentally retarded shall enroll not fewer than 10 nor more than 20 pupils per teacher, except as teacher aides are provided.

    In areas of high population density and mobility or where other extenuating circumstances prevail, the class size limitations may need to be revised downward to protect the interest of the individual pupil and the total school program.

2. (Administrative regulation) Teacher-pupil ratio shall be as follows at each school level:

Elementary:	Kindergarten	1:50
	Grades 1-3	1:30
	Grades 4-6	1:32
Intermediate:	Schools enrolling 600 or more pupils	1:27
	Schools enrolling fewer than 600 pupils	1:26
High Schools:	Schools enrolling 1,000 or more pupils	1:27
	Schools enrolling 800-999 pupils	1:26
	Schools enrolling fewer than 800 pupils	1:25

3. (Board policy) The optimum enrollment should be 25 pupils per class. The following maximum class sizes are set:

Kindergarten	30 pupils
Grades 1-3	31 pupils
Grades 4-5	33 pupils
Grade 6	35 pupils
Combination classes involving	
Grades 1-4	25 pupils
Grades 4-6	27 pupils

4. (Board regulation) As an over-all general policy, a membership of 30 pupils per class is accepted as a desirable maximum and 20 pupils per class is a desirable minimum, for all grade levels, with the following exceptions recognized:

Classes in physical education, typing, band, and vocal music will exceed the suggested maximum.

Classes for exceptional students, special adult groups, and certain vocational subjects will enroll fewer than the desired 20 pupils.

The size of a class taught by a team of two teachers will be approximately twice as large as one taught by a single teacher.

5. (Board regulation and salary schedule) Class size in secondary schools will be as follows:

English, social studies, general education, mathematics, science, language, business, art, and hygiene	27-33 pupils
Typing	30-40 pupils
Drafting	30 pupils
Vocational shops, homemaking, and industrial arts	22-24 pupils
Music (Grades 7-8)	54-66 pupils
Music (Grades 9-12)	35-40 pupils
Health education	45-60 pupils
Pool	30 pupils
Adapted classes	15-25 pupils
Occupational education	18 pupils
School work classes	25 pupils

6. (Guidelines; administrative regulations) "When a teacher assistant is assigned to help a classroom teacher with instructional duties, the size of the class may be adjusted proportionately to compensate for the additional staff. For staffing purposes, 20 hours of time devoted by teacher assistants shall be considered the equivalent of a full day of regular classroom teacher time."

7. (Board policy) The total teacher-pupil ratio shall not exceed:

Elementary	
1966-67	30.0
1967-68	29.1
Intermediate	
1966-67	23.0
1967-68	22.3
Secondary	
1966-67	22.0
1967-68	21.5

Arriving at Class Size Policy

One section of Ross and McKenna's publication (70) concerned "Class Size Policy and How It Is Made." The authors cite two major studies in this area.

The first study, conducted by Stover in 1954 (76), dealt in part with the process of determining class size. Ross and McKenna reported that "a number of the factors discovered by Stover as influencing class-size decisions have no justification in, or relation to, any intrinsic, empirical merits of the question." Instead, Stover concluded, "class-size policy in most school districts is a matter of expediency." "Class-size policies," Ross and McKenna reported, "are developed locally and are not influenced measurably by outside agencies, research, or practice in other districts. Birth-rate cycles, finance, and physical facilities have more often than not been the deciding factors." (70:14)

Furthermore, "class-size policy is much different in the living than in the verbalization." (70:14) "Adherence to policy, Stover found, is even more erratic than the factors taken into account when determining policy. Administrators use stated goals as generalizations, permitting wide deviations in size in actual practice as long as central tendency is maintained close to the desired point." (70:15)

The 1954 study by the New Rochelle (New York) School Study Council and the New Rochelle P.T.A. (60), which Ross and McKenna also cited, "indicates that community traditions are stable forces which tenaciously hold up concepts of reasonable class size." Findings in this study indicated that "communities in general are willing to build new buildings, rent church basements, and even go on half-sessions before departing too markedly from an established class-size policy." (70:16)

In this study, more than 70 local school administrators were asked to rate as "good," "harmless," "bad," or "very bad" 12 commonly used arrangements for handling increased enrollments while preserving reasonable and fairly uniform class size. In addition, the administrators were asked to indicate whether or not their school system had used the practice. Results showed a "low correlation between the desirability ratings given to the practices by administrators and their reported frequency of usage." (70:17)

Teacher/School Board Negotiations on Class Size

Written agreements in teacher/school board negotiations have increased in interest and in practice during recent years. Among the elements of the instructional program being negotiated is pupil-staff ratio and class size. The NEA Research Division publication, Negotiation Agreement Provisions, 1966-67 Edition, 7/ listed 222 current Level IV, or comprehensive, agreements which were on file in the Research Division depository of agreements on June 20, 1967, and which contain some sort of provision regarding class size and pupil-teacher ratio.

Examples of provisions in these written negotiations are given below.

1. Newark (N.J.) Board of Education and Newark Teachers' Association

Duration: February 1, 1967--February 1, 1970

"The Board and the Association agree to the following priority objectives:

1. Kindergarten classes shall have a maximum of twenty-five (25) pupils per teacher and all other regular classes shall have a maximum of thirty (30) pupils per teacher;..."

2. Stratford (Conn.) Board of Education and Stratford Education Association

Duration: February 15, 1966--September 1, 1968

"A.1. By the beginning of the 1966-67 school year, the maximum number of pupils per teacher shall be as follows:

Kindergarten and First Grade Classes   30
Traditional Classes (both in elementary and secondary schools*)   35
Special Education Classes   15

___
*The term "secondary schools" includes both junior high and senior high schools.

___
7/ National Education Association, Research Division. Negotiation Agreement Provisions, 1966-67 Edition. Washington, D.C.: the Association, October 1967. 406 p.

The term 'Traditional Classes' shall not include study halls, team teaching or physical education classes.

2. The Board and the Association agree that further reductions in class size limitations set forth above are desirable, and to the extent possible under the circumstances (e.g., availability of staff and facilities) such reductions shall be made.

B. No teacher shall be assigned responsibility for more than seventy-five (75) pupils at any moment in time.

C. The provisions of Sections A or B above may be modified only if the Superintendent of Schools determines that it is necessary to do so. The Association shall be notified in writing of each instance in which the Superintendent has so determined. A disagreement over whether an exception is justified shall be subject to the grievance procedure and shall be initiated at Level Two thereof."

3. The Board of Education of the City of Chicago and the Chicago Teachers Union

Duration: January 1, 1967--December 31, 1967

"8-1. Goals. In relation to class size, the BOARD has established as goals:

8-1.1. Based on the needs of the pupils, an average class size in elementary schools of 30 for approximately one-fourth of the city-wide enrollment, of 25 for approximately one-half of the city-wide enrollment, and of 20 for approximately one-fourth of the city-wide enrollment.

8-1.2. A pupil-teacher ratio in the general high school of 20; in the vocational high school of 18; and in the technical high school of 19.

8-2. Present Standards.

8-2.1. In the elementary schools, except when there is no space available or a large class size is necessary or desirable for a particular type of instruction, class size shall not exceed the currently established average class size of 33 by more than 15 to 20 percent.

8-2.2. In the high school, except when there is no space available, or a larger class is necessary or desirable for a particular type of instruction, or where there is a single section class, the class size shall not exceed 36. In classes such as English, where efforts by the BOARD have reduced maximums below this figure, every effort shall be made to continue this progress.

8-2.3. The number of pupils in laboratory, shop, and drafting classes shall not exceed the number of stations, tables, benches, or other work areas available.

8-2.4. The class size in special education classes shall be in accordance with guidelines established by the BOARD."

4. Lansing (Mich.) Schools Education Association, Inc. and Board of Education of Lansing School District, Ingraham, Eaton, and Clinton Counties, Michigan

Duration: September 6, 1966--June 30, 1969

"Whenever possible under the circumstances (availability of facilities and financial resources) the maximum number of pupils per teacher shall be as follows:

A. <u>Secondary Schools</u>

The maximum shall be 150 students per day except in special education, typing, physical education, music, and study hall unless otherwise required by law for the 1966-67 school year. Maximums for subsequent years shall be negotiated commencing March 1 of each year. This procedure will go into effect the second semester of the 1966-67 school year in the senior high schools. The junior high schools will adopt this procedure in the fall of 1967. The official enrollment count shall be determined as of Friday, the ninth week of each semester.

B. <u>Elementary Schools</u>

(1) Kindergarten   30
(2) First-Second Grade   26
(3) Third-Sixth Grade   30
(4) Combination Grades will be
    eliminated by the fall of
    1967 wherever possible   25
(5) Special Education   15
(6) The Board will continue to make every effort to service the disadvantaged areas with additional teaching staff.
(7) The official enrollment count shall be determined as of Friday, the ninth week of each semester.

This procedure will go into effect the second semester of the 1966-67 school year in the elementary schools.

In the establishment of experimental education programs involving large group instruction with a high pupil-teacher ratio the limits specified in Paragraphs A and B of this Article shall not apply, but such program shall not be established without mutual agreement between the LSEA Board of Directors and the Board."

5. The Board of Education of the City of New York and the United Federation of Teachers, Local 2, American Federation of Teachers

Duration: July 1, 1967--September 7, 1969

"6. Class Size Limitations

a. Pre-Kindergarten and Kindergarten

The size of pre-kindergarten classes shall be determined on the basis of a maximum of fifteen pupils for each teacher, except as specified in d. below.

The size of kindergarten classes shall be determined on the basis of a maximum of 25 pupils for each teacher, except as specified in d. below.

b. Elementary, Junior High, and High Schools

No subject class in elementary school shall exceed 33 pupils in the 1967-68 school year and 32 pupils in the 1968-69 school year, except as specified in d. below.

No subject class in non-special service junior high school shall exceed 33 pupils, except as specified in d. below.

No subject class in a special service junior high school shall exceed 33 pupils in the 1967-68 school year and 30 pupils in the 1968-69 school year, except as specified in d. below.

No subject class in senior high school shall exceed 36 pupils in the 1967-68 school year and 34 pupils in the 1968-69 school year, except as specified in d. below.

No class in trade shop subjects in the high schools shall exceed 29 pupils in the 1968-69 school year, except as specified in d. below.

The size of physical education classes in the high schools shall be determined on the basis of a maximum of 60 pupils for each teacher, except as specified in d. below.

The size of required music classes in the high schools shall be determined on the basis of a maximum of 50 pupils for each teacher, except as specified in d. below.

The reduction of class size to 34 in the school year 1968-69 in the high schools shall not be accomplished by an increase in the size of classes for the non-college bound students which prevailed in the 1967-68 school year.

The size of ninth grade classes in any high school where more than half of the pupils in the ninth grade have been admitted from reorganized junior high schools shall not exceed the maximum provided above for the junior high schools.

   c. '600' Schools.

No class in any '600' day school shall exceed 15 pupils, except as specified in d. below.

   d. Exceptions

An acceptable reason for exceeding the maximum class size limitations listed above may be any of the following:

   (1) There is no space available to permit scheduling of any additional class or classes in order to reduce class size.

   (2) Conformity to the class size objective would result in placing additional classes on short time schedule.

   (3) Conformity to the class size objective would result in the organization of half-classes.

   (4) A class larger than the maximum is necessary or desirable in order to provide for specialized or experimental instruction, or for IGC instruction, or for placement of pupils in a subject class of which there is only one on a grade.

In the event that it is necessary to assign a teacher to a class which exceeds the maximum size listed above, the principal shall stipulate the reason in writing to the teacher and to the Superintendent of Schools. Such statement of reasons may be available for examination by the Union in the office of the Superintendent of Schools.

6. Warwick (R.I.) School Committee and Warwick Education Association

Duration: February 1, 1967--January 31, 1969

"Wherever feasible under the circumstances (e.g., availability of staff and facilities), in both elementary schools (including kindergartens) and secondary schools (junior and senior high):

   1. The regular class shall be approximately 25 pupils, in accordance with the city's ability to provide school plants.

   2. The composition and size of Special Education classes shall be in accordance with State Laws.

   3. Classes containing concentrations of disadvantaged pupils shall be reduced in size as rapidly as practicable to a number which permits optimum learning opportunities for such pupils.

   4. The Committee and the Association agree that there should be a special arrangement for English teachers instructing composition, writing, and functional grammar to be responsible for 15 to 20 students per section to make a genuine contribution to quality education and to prepare students to cope with college demands.

The foregoing standards are subject to modification for educational purposes such as the avoidance of split-grade classes, or half-classes or specialized or experimental instruction (e.g., music, art, typing classes, physical education)."

7. The Board of Education of the School District of the City of Detroit (Mich.) and the Detroit Federation of Teachers

Duration: July 1, 1966--July 1, 1967

"The Union and the Administration acknowledge the desirability of reducing class size wherever possible as soon as funds are available for that purpose. In the interim, class size in regular classes throughout the system shall be as close as possible to the class size medians established during the 1965-66 school year. During the 1966-67 school year, the Board of Education shall do all within its power to hire a sufficient number of qualified teachers so that the class size medians shall not exceed the medians established during the 1965-66 school year."

(The contract negotiated in the fall of 1967 following the Detroit teachers' strike sets maximum class size at 38 in general, and at 30 for grades one through three in 50 inner-city schools. [19])

8. Board of Education of the City School District of Rochester, New York and the Rochester Teachers Association

Duration: July 1, 1967--June 30, 1968

"1. CLASS SIZE

Every effort will be made to adhere to the lower limit of the class size ranges set forth below. Classes larger than the maximum must be approved by the Administrative Director and a disagreement over whether such an exception is justified shall be subject to the procedures set forth in Section XI which shall be initiated at Level Two thereof.

   a. The class size of the Kindergarten and elementary school grades will be 27-33 pupils.

b. The following Special Education classes will adhere to the maximum numbers prescribed by State regulations or recommendations:

Educable Mentally Retarded Classes	15 pupils
Severely Mentally Retarded Classes	
Primary	12 pupils
Intermediate	12 pupils
Advanced	15 pupils
Orthopedic Classes	10-15 pupils
Sight Saving Classes	10-15 pupils
Hearing Conservation Classes	10-15 pupils

The following Special Education Classes for slow learners adhere to local regulations:

Ungraded Classes	18 pupils
Emotionally Disturbed Classes	8-10 pupils

c. Class size in secondary schools will be as follows:

English ....)	
Social Studies ....)	
General Education ....)	
Mathematics ....)	27-31 pupils
Science ....)	
Language ....)	
Business ....)	
Typing	30-40 pupils
Industrial Arts	22-24 pupils
Drafting	30 pupils
Vocational Shops	22-24 pupils
Home Economics	22-24 pupils
Music (Grades 7-8)	54-66 pupils
Music (Grades 9-12)	35-40 pupils
Art	27-33 pupils
Health Education	45-50 pupils
Pool	30 pupils
Hygiene	27-33 pupils
Adapted Classes	15-25 pupils
Occupational Education Classes	18 pupils
School Work Classes	25 pupils"

References

1. American Association of School Administrators. *Your AASA in Nineteen Sixty-Five--Sixty-Six*. Washington, D. C.: the Association, a department of the National Education Association, 1966. 256 p.

2. American Association of School Administrators. *Your AASA in Nineteen Sixty-Six--Sixty-Seven*. Washington, D. C.: the Association, a department of the National Education Association, 1967. 208 p.

3. American Association of School Administrators, Commission on School Buildings. *Schools for America*. Washington, D. C.: the Association, a department of the National Education Association, 1967. 175 p.

4. Anderson, Frank H., and others. "A Report of an Experiment at Camelback High School." *Mathematics Teacher* 56: 155-59; March 1963.

5. Anderson, Kenneth E. "The Relationship Between Teacher Load and Student Achievement." *School Science and Mathematics* 50: 468-70; June 1950.

6. Association for Supervision and Curriculum Development. "Resolutions." *ASCD News Exchange* 15: 13-16; April 1963.

7. Beggs, David W., III. *Decatur-Lakeview High School: A Practical Application of the Trump Plan*. Englewood Cliffs, N. J.: Prentice-Hall, 1964. 266 p.

8. Besvinick, Sidney L. "Scheduling Problems: How Many? How Long?" *Clearing House* 39: 425-27; March 1965.

9. Binion, Stuart. *An Analysis of the Relationship of Pupil-Teacher Ratio to School Quality*. Doctor's thesis. New York: Teachers College, Columbia University, 1954.

10. Blake, Howard V. *Class Size: A Summary of Selected Studies in Elementary and Secondary Schools*. Doctor's thesis. New York: Teachers College, Columbia University, 1954. 119 p.

11. Bovard, Everett W., Jr. "The Psychology of Classroom Interaction." *Journal of Educational Research* 45: 215-24; November 1951.

12. Cammarosano, Joseph R., and Santopolo, Frank A. "Teaching Efficiency and Class Size." *School and Society* 86: 338-41; September 27, 1958.

13. Cannon, Gwendolyn McConkie. "Kindergarten Class Size--A Study." *Childhood Education* 43: 9-11; September 1966.

14. Clark, Edwin C. *International Studies in Class Size*. Research No. 90. Burbank, Calif.: Burbank Unified School District, March 1, 1963. 6 p.

15. Clarke, S. C. T., and Richel, Sandra. *The Effect of Class Size and Teacher Qualifications on Achievement*. Research Monograph No. 5. Edmonton, Canada: Alberta Teachers' Association, April 1963. 71 p.

16. Cohen, Dorothy H. "Dependency and Class Size." *Childhood Education* 43: 16-19; September 1966.

17. Coleman, James S., and others. *Equality of Educational Opportunity*. U. S. Department of Heath, Education, and Welfare, Office of Education, Washington, D. C.: Government Printing Office, 1966. 737 p.

18. Croft Educational Services. "Legislation: Poverty Director Shriver Calls for 'Project Keep Moving.'" *Education Summary*, April 1, 1967. p. 4.

19. Croft Educational Services. "Trends and Issues: What Did Teachers Gain?" *Education Summary*, October 15, 1967. p. 1.

20. Doherty, James. "Pupil-Teacher Ratio in Head Start Centers." *Childhood Education* 43: 7-8; September 1966.

21. Fox, David J. *Expansion of the More Effective School Program*. New York: Center for Urban Education, September 1967. 124 p.

22. Frymier, Jack R. "The Effect of Class Size upon Reading Achievement in First Grade." *Reading Teacher* 18: 90-93; November 1964.

23. Goldstein, William. "Large Group Instruction: Boon or Bust?" *Clearing House* 40: 520-22; May 1967.

24. Hamilton, Jack A., and Madgic, Robert F. "Can Flexible Scheduling Improve Social Studies Instruction?" *Journal of Secondary Education* 39: 295-98; November 1964.

25. Harap, Henry. "Many Factors Affect Teacher Morale." *Nation's Schools* 63: 55-57; June 1959.

26. Haskell, Simon. "Some Observations on the Effects of Class Size upon Pupil Achievement in Geometrical Drawing." *Journal of Educational Research* 58: 27-30; September 1964.

27. Holland, Howard K., and Galfo, Armand J. *An Analysis of Research Concerning Class Size*. Research Contribution to Educational Planning, Number II. Richmond, Va.: State Department of Education, Division of Educational Research, November 1964. 21 p.

28. Hopper, Harold H., and Keller, Helen. "Teaching Writing Skills in Large Classes." *Junior College Journal* 37: 41-43; November 1966.

29. Jackson, Joe L. *School Size and Program Quality in Southern High Schools*. Nashville, Tenn.: Center for Southern Education Studies, George Peabody College for Teachers, 1966. 59 p.

30. Johnson, Robert H., and Lobb, M. Delbert. "Jefferson County, Colorado, Completes Three-Year Study of Staffing, Changing Class Size, Programming, and Scheduling." *Bulletin of the National Association of Secondary-School Principals* 45: 57-77; January 1961.

31. Keliher, Alice V. "Effective Learning and Teacher-Pupil Ratio." *Childhood Education* 43: 3-6; September 1966.

32. Lane, Mary B. "Creative Thinking on Critical Needs of Children." *Childhood Education* 43: 30-39; September 1966.

33. Leton, Donald A. "Group Processes: Some Implications in the Field of Education." *Education* 73: 135-40; October 1952.

34. Levin, Henry M. "The Coleman Report: What Difference Do Schools Make?" *Saturday Review* 51: 57-58, 66-67; January 20, 1968.

35. McKenna, Bernard. *Measures of Class Size and Numerical Staff Adequacy Related to a Measure of School Quality*. Doctor's thesis. New York: Teachers College, Colubia University, 1955.

36. Madden, Joseph V. *An Experimental Study of Student Achievement in General Mathematics in Relation to Class Size*. Doctor's thesis. Tempe: Arizona State University, 1966. 91 p. Abstract: *Dissertation Abstracts* 27: 631A-632A; No. 3, 1966.

37. Menniti, Daniel J. *A Study of the Relationship Between Class Size and Pupil Achievement in the Catholic Elementary School*. Doctor's thesis. Washington, D. C.: Catholic University of America, 1964. 110 p. Abstract: *Dissertation Abstracts* 25: 2854-55; No. 5, 1964.

38. Middle States Association of Colleges and Secondary Schools, Commission on Secondary Schools. *Bulletin of Information*. Philadelphia, Pa.: the Association, January 15, 1965. 4 p.

39. Miller, Richard I. *Education in a Changing Society*. Washington, D. C.: National Education Association, Project on the Instructional Program of the Public Schools, 1963. 166 p.

40. National Education Association. *NEA Handbook, 1967-68*. Washington, D. C.: the Association, August 1967. 416 p.

41. National Education Association, Department of Classroom Teachers. *Official Report, 1966-1967*. Washington, D. C.: the Department, 1967. 128 p.

42. National Education Association, Department of Elementary-Kindergarten-Nursery Education. "EKNE Passes Resolution on Early Childhood Services." <u>Keeping up with Early Education</u> 12: 6; September 1966.

43. National Education Association, Department of Elementary-Kindergarten-Nursery Education. "Resolutions." <u>Keeping up with Early Education</u> 9: 4; September 1963.

44. National Education Association, Department of Elementary-Kindergarten-Nursery Education. "Resolutions." <u>Keeping up with Early Education</u> 11: 6-7; September 1965.

45. National Education Association, Department of Elementary-School Principals. "1954-1962 Resolutions." <u>National Elementary Principal</u> 42: 33-48; January 1963.

46. National Education Association, Department of Elementary-School Principals. "Resolutions: Class and School Size." <u>National Elementary Principal</u> 46: 66; September 1966.

47. National Education Association, National Commission on Teacher Education and Professional Standards. <u>Manual for State and Local TEPS Commissions</u>. 1959 edition. Washington, D. C.: the Commission, 1959. 91 p.

48. National Education Association, Office of Professional Development and Welfare. <u>Profiles of Excellence: Recommended Criteria for Evaluating the Quality of a Local School System</u>. Washington, D. C.: the Association, 1966. 126 p.

49. National Education Association, Research Division. <u>The American Public-School Teacher, 1965-66</u>. Research Report 1967-R4. Washington, D. C.: the Association, 1967. 102 p. Stock #435-13310. $2.

50. National Education Association, Research Division. <u>Class Size in Kindergartens and Elementary Schools, March 1965</u>. Research Report 1965-R11. Washington, D. C.: the Association, July 1965. 28 p. (Out of print.) <u>Summary</u>: National Education Association, Research Division. "Class Size in Elementary Schools." <u>NEA Research Bulletin</u> 43: 106-109; December 1965.

51. National Education Association, Research Division. <u>Class Size in Secondary Schools, January 1964</u>. Research Report 1964-R16. Washington, D. C.: the Association, December 1964. 30 p. (Out of print.) <u>Summary</u>: National Education Association, Research Division. "Class Size in Secondary Schools." <u>NEA Research Bulletin</u> 43: 19-23; February 1965. <u>Summary</u>: Maul, Ray C. "How Large Are High School Classes?" <u>Bulletin of the National Association of Secondary-School Principals</u> 49: 103-13; January 1965.

52. National Education Association, Research Division. <u>Head Start Programs Operated by Public School Systems, 1966-67</u>. Research Report 1968-R3. Washington, D. C.: the Association, 1968. 42 p. $1. Stock #135-13346.

53. National Education Association, Research Division. "What Do Teachers Think?" <u>NEA Research Bulletin</u> 40: 120-25; December 1962.

54. National Education Association, Research Division and American Association of School Administrators. <u>Class Size in Large School Systems, 1966-67</u>. Educational Research Service Circular No. 4, 1967. Washington, D. C.: the Association, July 1967. 24 p.

55. National Education Association and American Association of School Administrators, Educational Policies Commission. <u>Contemporary Issues in Elementary Education</u>. Washington, D. C.: the Commission, 1960. 27 p.

56. National Education Association and American Association of School Administrators, Educational Policies Commission. <u>Education and the Disadvantaged American</u>. Washington, D. C.: the Commission, 1962. 39 p.

57. National Education Association and American Association of School Administrators, Educational Policies Commission. <u>An Essay on Quality in Public Education</u>. Washington, D. C.: the Commission, 1959. 29 p.

58. National School Public Relations Association. "Historic Study Attacked, Analyzed." <u>Education U. S. A.</u>, September 11, 1967. p. 7.

59. Newell, Clarence Albert. *Class Size and Adaptability*. Contributions to Education, No. 894. New York: Teachers College, Columbia University, 1943. 99 p.

60. New Rochelle School Study Council and New Rochelle P.T.A. Council Joint Committee. *Meeting Increased Enrolments--Plans Other Than Increasing Class Sizes*. New York: Metropolitan School Study Council, 1955.

61. North Central Association of Colleges and Secondary Schools. "Policies and Criteria for the Approval of Secondary Schools." *North Central Association Quarterly* 41: 147-62; Summer 1966.

62. Northwest Association of Secondary and Higher Schools, Commission on Secondary Schools. *Manual of Accrediting Secondary Schools*. Eugene, Oreg.: the Association (F. L. Stetson, Executive Secretary-Treasurer, University of Oregon), 1962. 15 p.

63. Otte, Roy W. "Creativity in Teaching." *Childhood Education* 43: 40-43; September 1966.

64. Otto, Henry J., and von Borgersrode, Fred. "Class Size." *Encyclopedia of Educational Research*. Revised edition. New York: Macmillan Co., 1950. p. 212-16.

65. Otto, Henry J., and others. *Class Size Factors in Elementary Schools*. Bureau of Laboratory Schools Publication No. 4. Austin: University of Texas, 1954. 178 p.

66. Pertsch, C. Frederick. "Some Effects of Class Size on the Educational Program in New York City Elementary Schools." *The Advancing Front of Education*. Eighth Yearbook, New York Society for the Experimental Study of Education. New York: Thesis Publishing Co., 1943. p. 3-21.

67. Pugh, James B. *The Performance of Teachers and Pupils in Small Classes*. Metropolitan School Study Council, Commission on the School of 1980, Commission Study No. 1. New York: Institute of Administrative Research, Teachers College, Columbia University, 1965. 41 p.

68. Richman, Harold. *Educational Practices as Affected by Class Size*. Doctor's thesis. New York: Teachers College, Columbia University, 1955.

69. Rohrer, John H. "Large and Small Sections in College Classes." *Journal of Higher Education* 28: 275-79; May 1957.

70. Ross, Donald H., and McKenna, Bernard. *Class Size: The Multi-Million Dollar Question*. Published by the Institute of Administrative Research, for the Metropolitan School Study Council, with the sponsorship of the New York State Council of School Superintendents. New York: Institute of Administrative Research, Teachers College, Columbia University, 1955. 24 p.

71. Senate Factfinding Committee on Governmental Administration. *Let Us Teach: Final Report on an Analysis of the Helpfulness of Certain Aspects of the School Program to Classroom Teaching*. A Report of the Senate Factfinding Committee on Governmental Administration. Sacramento: Senate of the State of California, 1965. 56 p.

72. Shane, Harold G. "What Research Says About Class Size and Human Development." *NEA Journal* 50: 30-32; January 1961.

73. Southern Association of Colleges and Schools. *Proceedings: 71st Annual Meeting, Miami Beach, Fla*. Atlanta, Ga.: the Association (Suite 592, 795 Peachtree Street, N.E., 30308), 1967. 335 p.

74. Southern Association of Colleges and Schools, Joint Study Committee of Commission on Secondary Schools and Commission on Research and Service. *The Junior High School Program*. Atlanta, Ga.: the Association (795 Peachtree Street, N.E., Atlanta 8), 1958. 112 p.

75. Stevenson, P. R. *Smaller Classes or Larger; A Study of the Relation of Class Size to the Efficiency of Teaching*. Journal of Educational Research Monograph No. 4, 1923. Bloomington, Ill.: Public School Publishing Co., 1923. 127 p.

76. Stover, Frank B. *Administrative Policies on Class Size*. Doctor's thesis. New York: Teachers College, Columbia University, 1954.

77. Trump, J. Lloyd. *Images of the Future*. Urbana, Ill.: Commission on the Experimental Study of the Utilization of the Staff in the Secondary Schools, 1959. 46 p.

78. Vincent, William S.; McKenna, Bernard H.; and Swanson, Austin D. "The Question of Class Size." IAR Research Bulletin 1: 1-4; October 1960.

79. Warburton, John T. "An Experiment in Large Group Instruction." Journal of Secondary Education 36: 430-32; November 1961.

80. Whitsitt, Robert C. Comparing the Individualities of Large Secondary School Classes with Small Secondary School Classes Through the Use of a Structured Observation Schedule. Doctor's thesis. New York: Teachers College, Columbia University, 1955.

81. Williams, Homer R., and Koelsche, Charles L. "Organization of Chemistry Classes." Science Teacher 34: 52-54; May 1967.

Research Reports

1967-R4	The American Public-School Teacher, 1965-66. 102 p. $2.00. #435-13310.
1967-R5	Leaves of Absence for Classroom Teachers, 1965-66. 61 p. $1.25. #435-13312.
1967-R6	The Teacher's Day in Court: Review of 1966. 60 p. $1.25. #435-13314.
1967-R7	The Pupil's Day in Court: Review of 1966. 61 p. $1.25. #435-13316.
1967-R9	Faculty Salary Schedules for Public Community-Junior Colleges, 1965-66: A Pilot Study of 2-Year Institutions. 45 p. $1.00. #435-13320.
1967-R10	Formal Grievance Procedures for Public-School Teachers, 1965-66. 63 p. $1.25. #435-13322.
1967-R11	23rd Biennial Salary Survey of Public-School Professional Personnel, 1966-67: National Data. 36 p. $1.00. #435-13324.
1967-R12	23rd Biennial Salary Survey of Public-School Professional Personnel, Data for Systems with Enrollments of 12,000 or More. 259 p. $3.75. #435-13326.
1967-R13	High Spots in State School Legislation, January 1 - August 31, 1967. 105 p. $2.50. #435-13328.
1967-R14	Faculty Salary Schedules in Colleges and Universities, 1965-66: A Pilot Study of Institutions Granting the 4-Year Bachelor's or Higher Degree. 42 p. $1.00. #435-13330.
1967-R16	Salary Schedules for Teachers, 1967-68. 103 p. $2.50. #435-13334.
1967-R17	Evaluation of Teacher Salary Schedules, 1966-67 and 1967-68. 133 p. $3.00. #435-13336.
1967-R18	Teacher Supply and Demand in Public Schools, 1967. 88 p. $1.75. #435-13338.
1967-R19	Estimates of School Statistics, 1967-68. 36 p. $1.00. #435-13340.
1968-R1	Rankings of the States, 1968. 71 p. $1.25. #435-13342.
1968-R2	Salary Schedules for Administrative Personnel, 1967-68. 97 p. $2.00. #435-13344.
1968-R3	Head Start Programs Operated by Public School Systems, 1966-67. 42 p. $1.00. #435-13346.
1968-R4	Economic Status of the Teaching Profession, 1967-68. 56 p. $1.25. #435-13348.
1968-R5	Salary Schedules for Principals, 1967-68. 126 p. $2.50. #435-13350.
1968-R6	Nursery School Education, 1966-67. 48 p. $1.00. #435-13352.

Research Summaries

1966-S1	Inservice Education of Teachers. 19 p. 60¢. #434-22802.
1966-S2	Homework. 12 p. 30¢. #434-22804.
1967-S1	School Dropouts. 55 p. 75¢. #434-22808.
1968-S2	Class Size. 49 p. $1.00. #434-22810.